Ali,

Keep Striving,

thriving +

winning! -

Best

You can't fake passion. Curtiss Jacobs is the living embodiment of that statement. When you find yourself wrestling in the mosh pit of the current corporate landscape, desperately searching for clarity and a viable path forward, reach for this book. Curtiss's infectious smile, sharp mind, and genuine warmth come through, and after only a few pages you will realize that you've just covered more ground—and with more depth—than most paid intellectuals on the talk show circuit. Curtiss's passion for humanity, justice, and economic equity is boundless and only tempered by his genuine love of people, whether he is serving in the role of corporate executive, community mentor, or friend. His ability to remain transparent and egoless as a senior leader in a major Fortune 500 firm—while operating under the relentless strain of aggressive productivity and profitability objectives and simultaneously putting his team's best professional interests first—is not only uncommon in a profit-driven landscape but also his most easily identifiable trait. Curtiss runs on a high-grade fuel. What is this energy source that propels him to seek his personal best while first promoting and encouraging others? Passion. It can't be faked.

—SUSAN MIDDLETON, corporate survivor

I credit Curtiss Jacobs with helping me not only understand my brand but also my holistic identity (which a brand is part of). He positions these two essentials for life in the corporate world as something you nurture and guard against invasive energy from society, corporate America, etc., and this book shows you how. Curtiss's leadership philosophy can be summed up in a few quotes, such as "I am not my job" and "If I got fired today, my identity would not cease to exist with the job title." He emphasizes the importance of having goals and passions outside of work so you remain a whole person. It's important to use the resources and tools of corporate America to build your "tool kit" for life after work or entrepreneurial adventures in parallel to building your career, and in this book, Curtiss clears the path for you to do so.

—MATTHEW LUNDY, banking vice president

I very much enjoyed reading this book. Curtiss has a frank, matter-of-fact style that's backed by real experience (aka wisdom), which makes the read feel light and informative. Although Curtiss is clearly Black and provides advice for people of color, the book isn't limited to a "Black man's" perspective on corporate America. There's a lot of advice in this book, and the tone is great. Curtiss straddles the line of being positive when appropriate while showing real-world examples of negativity. You will appreciate his honesty about his failures—many of which he reflected on and turned into gains—and the power mapping of organizations so you can best understand "the Game." That approach is very strategic to networking, promotions, efficiency, and success.

—JORDAN STOCKDALE,
New York City Mayor's Office

The book is masterfully written and eminently readable. Curtiss Jacob's leadership philosophy comes shining through. No boring "frameworks" here. It is the avuncular wisdom of someone who respects the priorities of business while caring deeply about the people who are expected to get the work done and produce the desired results. The book is also sensitively written. Its pragmatic logic breaks down the component pieces of organizational success and challenges the reader to first find strength from within. Curtiss includes excellent and varied personal stories, lists, and examples throughout. Few authors have the finesse to mention capitalism, historical trauma, and Luke 12:48 in a single paragraph and have the reader come away thinking, "Yes, I can." This book comprehensively covers topics of concern for aspiring professionals attempting to make their way through the corporate thicket of selfish-interests, fragile egos, and unreasonable expectations. Curtiss demystifies the journey by shining a bright light along the path.

—VERNA FORD, executive coach,
Ford Consulting & Coaching, LLC

I genuinely enjoyed this book. In this day and age of beating a dead horse by staying on one subject too long, Curtiss does the opposite, which makes for a seamless read. The book and its cultural references made me laugh and also think. *Demystifying Corporate America* is insightful but cautious not to minimize people's feelings. The HR section is so spot-on. The interviews scattered throughout provide excellent context and the "reason for being" chart is be beyond insightful. Overall, this is a book I highly recommend and keep in my collection.

—RICHARD WELSH, corporate managing director

DEMYSTIFYING
CORPORATE
AMERICA

DEMYSTIFYING CORPORATE AMERICA

A Real World Guide on Navigating the Corporate Landscape Without Losing Your Personal Life, Your Mind, or Your Soul

CURTISS JACOBS

Demystifying Corporate America: A Real World Guide on Navigating the Corporate Landscape Without Losing Your Personal Life, Your Mind, or Your Soul

This book is a work of non-fiction. Unless otherwise noted, the author and the publisher make no explicit guarantees as to the accuracy of the information contained in this book. In some cases, names of individuals and places have been altered to protect their privacy.

For information about this title or to order other books and/or electronic media, contact the publisher:

Kuelimika Publishing
2075 Seventh Avenue
New York City, NY 10027
www.curtissjacobs.com
hello@curtissjacobs.com

ISBNs:
979-8-9858780-0-4 (hardcover)
979-8-9858780-1-1 (softcover)
979-8-9858780-2-8 (eBook)

Library of Congress Control Number: 2022905966

Printed in the United States of America

Cover and interior design: 1106 Design
Editorial work: Christina Palaia, Emerald Editorial Services

Because of the dynamic nature of the internet, any web address or links referenced in this book may have changed since publication and may no longer be valid.

This book is written honoring the memories of
My father, Joseph David Jacobs
My grandparents, David Jacobs, Curtis and
Zain Beckett, Robert and Ruth Birch
My parents of the heart, Joseph and Rosemary Fisher
My nephew of the heart, Benjamin Allen Fisher Jr.
My sister of the heart, Roxanna Floyd
My dear friends Kirk Foster Collins Sr. and Lanette Winford
Colleagues, Joseph Benniefield Jr. and Manal Lopez
Mentors William Simmons, Dr. Earl Mosely, Richard Avedon,
and John Vandenberg

This book is dedicated to
My mother Earthell
My wife Camille
My siblings Ralph and Zain

▪ ▪ ▪

My daughters Tashii, Bria, Amber, and Tyler
My grandchildren Noni and Judah
My nieces Yannick, Imani, Zain-Minkah, and Yasmine
My nephew Menelik
My godchildren Niya, Tiffany, Olivia,
Lauren, Carlise, Ryan, and Liam
I hope that these pages will inspire them to have a career
and a life that are fulfilling and aligned to their purpose of being.

Contents

Contents

Foreword

can't begin to tell you how honored I felt when Curtiss Jacobs approached me with a request to contribute the foreword of his book. For the past almost twenty years, I've had a front-row seat in observing Curtiss astutely and deftly maneuver and matriculate up the corporate ladder. First encountering him when I was named President, U.S. Operations, at Pitney Bowes Management Services, I was immediately impressed not only with his professionalism and performance but also his intellectual curiosity and dedication to continuous learning. What I found most fascinating was his passion for connecting people and his hunger for wanting to know more about "how" to play and win in "the Game" of corporate America.

Demystifying Corporate America is without exception an honest and refreshing look at the challenges, pitfalls, and gamesmanship that many professionals fall victim to as they attempt to ascend the corporate ladder. Drawn from his experiences and observations gained over the course of his thirty-year career working in multiple industries, disciplines, and global geographies, Curtiss offers the reader a frank, matter-of-fact glimpse of how the Game is played. Most importantly, he offers insight and suggestions on how today's professional can captain their corporate destiny. Though it's second nature to many, Curtiss paints a vivid picture of what life is really like today in corporate America. He delivers a real-life conversation on understanding the importance of work–life balance, uncovers some of the "unknown" realities of corporate life, and inspires and encourages the reader to be intentional about their life and career.

After becoming one of his mentors, I was intrigued by the complexity of his background. Unlike many of his generation who transitioned from earning an undergraduate degree to earning a corporate paycheck, Curtiss's career journey took him down the road less traveled. Prior to beginning his corporate career as an entry-level hourly employee at Merrill Lynch, he spent time with the New York State Police and years as a professional photographer working with some of the world's top celebrities and publications. While such a background most certainly enhanced his ability to interact with various personalities, it left him less prepared to deal with the obstacles, politics, and flat-out double standards that exist in the meeting rooms of corporate America.

As a reader you may be asking, "What makes Curtiss an authority on this subject?" Well, I'm glad you asked. Though not fully prepared when he entered the corporate world (in particular, the world of Wall Street), Curtiss decided early on that he would not be a backseat driver when it came to his career. Taking to heart some advice that I shared as a mentor, he was determined to be the "owner, author, and architect" of his career. Analyzing everything from his appearance, communication style, interpersonal skills, and knowledge gaps, he set out to reinvent himself into a true corporate athlete. He invested in himself, from obtaining a bachelor's degree and later an MBA while working full-time at my suggestion (as not to let hiring managers use the lack of an MBA as an excuse to disqualify him from an opportunity), to honing a professional image and executive presence that took a backseat to no one. He became the epitome of the "5 Wells": well learned, well traveled, well dressed, well spoken, and well mannered!

In chapters just as clear and focused as his advice and writing style, Curtiss not only calls out organizations and bad characters for their hypocrisy, bigotry, and outright favoritism (while claiming to be a meritocracy) but also offers young professionals solutions and a road map to successfully navigate these landmines and be able to, in the words of Harvey B. Mackay, "swim with the sharks, without being eaten alive"! *Demystifying Corporate America* should be considered mandatory reading for college and university students, as well as any professional who wants to know the secrets to playing the Corporate Game successfully. One of my favorite chapters, "Get Smart about Money," is a must-read for everyone, as so many of us entered the workplace with little to no money management education.

After years of encouraging Curtiss to codify his wisdom and share it with the world, I am extremely proud of him and his dedication to mentoring others. Because of him, when I look at my mentoring tree, he has expanded it to include a new generation of leaders. Leaders who, just as Curtiss embraced my mentoring to soar to greater heights, will one day share his wisdom with generations to come. In closing, my relationship with Curtiss has grown from being a mentor, to being a peer, to now a brotherhood. It is my hope that the readers of *Demystifying Corporate America* will use this book as the foundation for watering their own mentoring tree!

—Keith R. Wyche
Author, *Diversity Is Not Enough*

Preface

've had double-Ivy-educated executives cry in my office because they were consistently being overlooked for growth opportunities, refused the same level of resources relative to their peers, layered by someone less qualified, and threatened by the talent level around them. They couldn't cope and sought my advice on how to be a contender in the Corporate Game. My executive assistants would work feverishly to pry open time in my calendar to accommodate so many colleagues who simply wanted guidance.

Once, a senior leader, a direct report of the CEO, said to me, "You would be really good at HR." My surprised response was, "Am I not good at what I'm doing now as an operations executive?" He laughed and said, "Of course you are, but you are very compassionate and good with people." I thought to myself, these people don't understand the importance of employee engagement. Driving business outcomes and caring for people are not mutually exclusive.

It was then that I looked around at the general disposition of my fellow corporate Americans and saw confusion, anguish, distress. Not that they didn't have talent, skills, credentials, and heart to build their careers on—they simply hadn't figured out the rules of the Game they were playing. Some didn't even realize they were playing a game.

It didn't have to be this way. I knew a few things that could help up-and-comers navigate the tricky waters of corporate America—after all, I'd weathered the storms of a corporate career by playing the Game as it was explained to me by the people controlling the chessboard.

During the COVID lockdowns, when fatalities were mounting, it hit me like a sledgehammer: Tomorrow is not promised. Aside from my mentees, executives I've coached, and former employees, who would even know that I existed in corporate America after I'm gone? My legacy would be totally dependent on word of mouth and those who remembered me.

I'd been thinking about writing a book for more than fifteen years. I hadn't done so because my schedule was so hectic with my job, my businesses, my board duties, and more. But as these commitments came to their natural close, I decided not to add more to my plate from the endless pipeline. I turned down investment opportunities that would have required too much of my focus as well as opportunities to serve a prestigious national not-for-profit as a board trustee.

Suddenly, I had time to collect my thoughts and put them in writing. For this book, I sat down and talked with peers who lead at the forefront of their fields. I spoke with my mentors as well as my mentees. I sifted through a trove of events and turning points in my own life on the long and twisting road of my corporate career. I've curated these insights to pass along to new corporate Americans as well as veterans of the Game so that you don't have to suffer while you work. When you have a clear view of the playing field, you have a much better chance of making a successful play.

I want to show you the Game you're in. I want you to realize your power to effect change. You can change the way the Game is played in corporate America just by participating. You won't mimic toxic behavior but will strive to be the change you want to see. Once you learn the rules of the Game, you'll see that you don't need to use others as a stepladder to the top, and neither will you let them trample over you for their own advantage.

You can instead be strategic and intentional about every aspect of your career plans *and* fit them neatly into your life plans.

Now, I don't want to see any more of you in my office frustrated over your chances. Read this book, learn the Game, and then go and have an experience that you can love while in corporate America.

Introduction

Many top business schools churn out talented individuals who can create a macro-laden spreadsheet or slick PowerPoint at a moment's notice. Personally, I would rather be led by someone who understands the human condition—in all its glory and struggle.

—Susan Leslie Middleton,
corporate survivor and friend

hope you're not seeking to find in these pages a detailed theoretical framework for managing your corporate career. If so, you've come to the wrong place. This is not a book of theory but a practical, experience-based guide on navigating the corporate landscape. Its purpose is to help you play—and win—the Corporate Game. Make no mistake, reaching the loftiest levels of corporate America *is* a game. You should approach it like you would a chessboard— assuming, of course, the Game is important to you.

After all, you're under no obligation to play.

I say this as someone who began his career as an artist—a player in the world of celebrity and fashion photography—who initially stepped onto the lowest rung of the corporate ladder for the medical benefits. I also say this as someone who has never *inextricably* tied his financial or career goals—much less his identity—to a particular job title or role, thanks to my roles as corporate executive, small business owner, and community activist. Finally, I say this as someone who knows how difficult it is to scale the ladder while remaining true to your core values. My perspective—and therefore this book—is based on my real-world experiences (and those of my colleagues) of what it takes to thrive in a hyper-competitive environment.

That path is not right for everyone. As the character Omar Little says in the HBO series *The Wire*, "But the game is out there, and it's either play or get played."

Over the past thirty years, I've played the Game across a variety of iconic companies and industries. During that time, I learned that pawns are viewed as plentiful, cheap, and disposable. And unfortunately, too often, so are leaders who lead with empathy and fairness. During my trek from entry-level job to senior executive, I've worked alongside colleagues and subordinates who've become good friends, close enough to count as extended family. These people have infused the best parts of themselves into their roles and treated their peers and subordinates with respect and kindness. Over the years, some managers and senior executives even went out of their way to shepherd my career.

But I've also worked with some truly horrible people. To paraphrase Obi-Wan Kenobi: You will never find a more wretched hive of amoral, self-dealing scum and villainy as you will in certain organizations and departments. I've seen executives who had everything to gain from treating their subordinates with courtesy behave like absolute assholes instead, vindictively destroying employees' careers and sense of self-worth. I've had to work with colleagues who were underqualified, overpromoted, and obnoxious. If not for the good ole boy network, some of these managers would not have been considered for an entry-level role in the mailroom.

Again, this is not the right career strategy for everyone, so be aware of what you're getting into before you play the Game.

Corporate America is staffed with the best and worst that humanity has to offer. The best people understand that the current system is rigged to benefit only a tiny fraction of the players, and some are sincerely working to change things. The worst don't understand this, don't care, or simply want to preserve their built-in advantages. Don't hold your breath waiting for the system to change. If you want change, *you* will have to make it happen.

There's No "Trick"

Ultimately, there's no "trick" to successfully climbing the corporate ladder while preserving your moral compass, sanity, and sense of mission. You simply need a certain level of self-awareness—a sense of who you are and where you come from. Armed with this awareness, you have everything you need to win the Game without becoming a tragic Greek hero in the process.

My self-awareness was recently bolstered by genealogy research. After doing some digging into the lives of my ancestors, I learned that my path was not an anomaly. It's one that many of my family members have followed. I come from a long line of creative people: entrepreneurs, politicians, social activists, and war veterans dating back to the American Revolution. I come from hardy stock:

from survivors of the Middle Passage, slavery, the Wilmington Insurrection of 1898 in North Carolina, and Jim Crow.

Knowing where you come from is incredibly empowering. When you know your history, you can draw on that knowledge as a source of strength and inspiration, and then push forward.

Keep this in mind as you learn how the Game works and what your strategic options are. Maintain an awareness of who you are, where you've been, and where you are today. You'll also derive a lot of value from pausing every now and then to spot the "mile markers" along the route and evaluate your experiences—good, bad, and mediocre.

Awareness is critical. As you play the Game, it's important to maintain a certain detachment, as if you were observing someone else. *Always remember who you are and that you're playing a game.* This will enable you to occasionally step outside yourself and dispassionately assess your mistakes, progress, and next steps. The greatest danger is that you'll become so absorbed by the Game that you'll lose your objectivity and allow events and emotions to carry you along like a dinghy caught in a tidal wave.

If you decide to play the Game, this book will help you develop not only your corporate brand but also a holistic identity (Chapter 3). You'll learn to recognize when someone is nurturing you while guarding against the negative aspects of corporate culture (Chapter 1). You'll develop the confidence to hold your head up after a misstep, even a major one, because trouble is not meant to last (Chapter 4). You are—and will always be—a work in progress.

Know that you are *not* your job. If you were fired today, your identity would not cease to exist, unless you allowed that to happen. Hence, the importance of developing serious goals and passions outside work (Chapter 7). If your goal is to reach the C-suite, that's wonderful. But perhaps you're the kind of person who plays the odds—who knows there are only about twelve hundred such jobs in the Fortune 100, fewer than the total number of roster spots as in the National Football League. Are those odds insurmountable? No. Are there other options? Yes.

Your journey needn't begin *and end* in the corporate world. Instead, your corporate career might comprise just a small slice of a larger pie, representing a time when you learned and built relationships while contributing to the company's success. All the while, you could position yourself to launch your own company, ministry, or community-based organization or to run for public office. The corporate experience that you gain will be valuable if you approach it with the right mindset. If you leverage your experience in corporate America as "R&D," you can apply the knowledge and resources gained there to build a "toolkit" for a life outside.

I hope this book gives leaders as well as aspiring leaders the confidence to hold your heads high regardless of the situation and to resist doing what's merely expedient instead of what's best for the organization, its employees, and the communities it serves. I hope you'll be inspired to walk the path of "egoless leadership," leveraging your skills, knowledge, and experiences to nurture the talents of your subordinates rather than treating them as potential threats. Most of all, I hope you'll recognize that progress is not a historical inevitability but something that requires human effort and leadership. If we're to overcome the challenges posed by climate change, discrimination, and inequality, we need the passion, determined efforts, and ingenuity of people like you. At the end of the day, mission statements and corporate pledges are nothing but words unless people like you are willing to actually pursue those missions and make good on those pledges.

Whether you've inherited historical trauma or historical wealth, you have a role to play. You can help ensure that corporations live up to their promises and make the world a better place, even as you earn a good living. The best way to get started is to determine what your value system is and then translate those values into a code of executive behavior. If capitalism is to survive, it will need leaders—leaders who are motivated by a sense of responsibility, duty, and mission, not just a desire for short-term "wins" and self-enrichment. We've had our fill of the latter over the last forty years. It's your generation's turn to demonstrate what *true leadership* looks like.

To whom much is given, much will be required.
—Luke 12:48

CHAPTER ONE

Caveat Operarius
(Employee Beware)

Few people would ever apply** for a position with a company called Evil Corp. Yet, at some point in your career, there's a good chance that you'll interview with an organization whose mission, vision, and core values don't align with yours. Although the firm may not deliberately seek to impoverish communities, destroy the environment, or crush the human spirit, a close examination of its culture, policies, and investments might uncover some unappetizing things. Before seeking employment at a new firm, therefore, it's important to do some research.

Before you interview, take the first (and obvious) step of visiting the company's website. Although the mission statement and About Us section will undoubtedly spin rose-tinted stories about everything the company does—from social responsibility and diversity programs to environmental stewardship—you might glean a few truths by reading between the lines.

For example: If the website boasts that "people are our most precious resource" or some such cliché, but another page touts the company's priorities as advancing digital technologies, it's a fairly good bet the company views people as less a "precious resource" than a fungible commodity, and that indeed is its right. The investments in workforce digitization are designed to connect people, places, and things with business processes to accelerate productivity. The collateral damage will be that certain roles and segments of the current workforce will no longer exist; it's simply a reality that you must be aware of. Remember, shareholders expect companies to create profits, not jobs.

Alternatively, compare what's written on the company's website with information you collect from other sources. It's one thing for (say) a financial services company to claim that it values diversity and the minority communities it serves but quite another to back up those claims with real money and sincere efforts to ensure that truly underrepresented minorities are represented at the most senior levels of the firm. What's posted on the company website doesn't always jibe with the decisions being made in the boardroom. The firm may have a diversity hiring program that it showcases to the media and community activists, but how much business is it *really* doing with minority-owned banks in local communities? Is senior management claiming to care about the environment while investing in fossil fuel stocks and contributing to the election campaigns of Senators Voldemort and Nosferatu?

To get the answers to these questions, dig deeper. Check out additional sources of news and information about the company. Consult with your personal network of friends and peers. What do they know about the company and its values and culture?

Do any of them have contacts in the organization? Have any of them worked there? Have they seen articles, blog posts, news releases, speeches, or videos in the news media or on social media about (or by) the firm's senior executives? What kinds of forecasts and promises have senior executives made in the past, and how do they compare with the realities later reported in the financial press or in annual reports? If your top priority is to join a fast-growing company, but the CEO's previous growth forecasts consistently fell short, you may want to reconsider that company. Do you really want to be led by people who routinely fail to deliver their promises?

Another way to learn what prospective employers are actually doing is to set up Google Alerts. Enter the name of the company and/or the names of some of its senior executives so that you'll receive alerts whenever one of them is in the news. Read what the company's leaders and employees are saying about it on LinkedIn or Fishbowl. And be sure to visit Glassdoor, a job and recruitment website that features millions of job listings, along with a database of company reviews, CEO approval ratings, salary reports, benefit reviews, and office photos provided by the employees of those firms.

I also recommend that you follow the organization's top executives on social media. Start following the CEO, C-suite executives, and board chairs of the firms you're interested in. These people are typically a company's mouthpiece. By staying current with what these leaders are saying, including presentations and reports, you'll be able to judge how well their statements match—or conflict with—the information on the company website.

Applying for a Job

Don't stop researching once you start interviewing. Instead, ask each interviewer a few questions to help you gather more "intel" on the nature of the company and its values. But be subtle. Although your goal should be to vet the company as well as it vets you, you don't want to come across as entitled—like someone who isn't interested in joining the company unless it meets a laundry list of nitpicky specifications. Phrase your questions like this:

- "What made you decide to come work for this company?"
- "What keeps you here? You've been here for __ years."
- "What are the biggest benefits of working here?"
- "Are there any challenges to working here?"

Most interviewers will respond with fuzzy platitudes, but a few may be honest—honest enough to make the exercise worthwhile. For example, some interviewers might respond by saying, "I once considered leaving the firm, but then realized that the problem was my manager, not the culture. And after my manager left . . ."

Even if you receive no honest answers, it can't hurt to ask.

You may also want to inquire about employee satisfaction and engagement surveys, especially when you're talking with HR representatives. Not every company surveys the workforce, but when they do, the results can say a lot about the company culture. Ask questions such as, "How have employee engagement scores been over the last three to five years? Are they trending in a positive direction, or have they been level or in decline? What are the main drivers?" (Negative drivers include poor compensation, few growth opportunities, and poor work–life balance.) If you don't receive straight answers, that, in itself, is very revealing.

Be mindful that the hiring manager may already have a preferred candidate in mind, perhaps someone from within their personal network or succession plan, or simply someone who is a "strong recommendation" from a senior leader stakeholder. If that's the case, you may have somewhat of an uphill battle in convincing them that you are the right person for the role, so your goal is to change their mind. How would you know if there's a preferred candidate? Just ask: *Has a preferred candidate already been identified?* Remember, interviews are two-way conversations, and that's a fair question. If the answer is yes, follow up with one or two of the following questions:

- What areas of my résumé drew you to me as a candidate?
- Is there a specific challenge not listed in the job description that you'll be looking to solve through the hiring of this role?
- What would success look like in the first six to twelve months for this role?
- Are there any glaring talent gaps within the organization that you are looking to address?
- What's the job grade and pay range associated with the role?

Then tailor your selling points to the interviewer's response.

Things to Be Mindful Of

Some companies will post a role and, unbeknownst to the job candidates, bring in candidates with deep subject matter experience as a way to conduct market research. This typically happens when the corporation is standing up a new capability and is not confident that the requisite skill sets exist internally. You'll find the hiring manager asking you questions like these:

- Tell me a bit about your role at company X.
- What was a day in the life like in that capacity?
- Explain to me how you leveraged the framework that you developed to solve critical issues for your stakeholders.
- What was the composition of your team? How many people did you manage? What were their levels and where did you fit in on your one-up manager's org chart?
- Explain to me a difficult challenge that you had to address, how you solved it, and how you communicated the outcome to senior leadership.

Answers to these questions from a dozen candidates provide a nice playbook that can then be handed to the eventual winner. The reality is the interviewer received advisory level input from industry leaders and didn't have to pay a dime.

Remember, the interview process is for you to gather enough information about the company and the job to decide whether you want to accept a role as much as it is for the interviewer to decide whether they want to offer you a role. Some companies whose push toward diversity and inclusion efforts extends to hiring require a diverse interview panel and a diverse slate of candidates. Be aware when you are the quota filler for that slate of candidates. Several indicators can tip you off:

- The interview panel has token representation from those who don't interact with the role you are interviewing for.
- The interview panel seems disinterested in your candidacy—the interview starts late and ends early, with no substantive discussion.
- You are being asked and recommended to interview for adjacent roles within the same organization that are loosely related to your skill set.

Understanding a company's culture is key to determining whether that company or department is the ideal fit for you. During the interview process, be intentional about asking specific questions about the organizational culture:

- How would you describe the company's culture?
- What personality types typically experience the most success here?
- What is your company's process for capturing and responding to employee feedback?
- Work–life balance means different things to different people. How would you define it?

Ask the same questions at every interview and keep a record of all responses for later review during your decision-making process.

While it's important that you are alert to organizational culture, be aware that your direct manager will have the biggest impact on your day-to-day satisfaction, or dissatisfaction, with your role. You'll want to understand the organizational rules this person operates under as well as their management style and nuanced behavioral patterns to be sure they align with yours. You could be looking for a manager to learn from who has no interest in teaching, or you could require autonomy to be your most productive, but have a micromanager. These characteristics of your direct manager will ultimately affect your performance.

If you are interviewing for a role where the manager has not been identified or has been identified but not announced, zero in on the characteristics of the manager who has been or is being recruited to assess how well their management style corresponds with your work style.

Where to Draw the Line

Everyone wants to work for an organization that strives to improve the lives of its employees, customers, and communities. At the same time, everyone has to eat and put a roof over their heads, and many also need to care for children. Depending on your financial circumstances and the state of the economy, you may not have the luxury of "delisting" a particular company from your prospects menu based on a values conflict. So, where do you draw the line between the need to earn a living and the desire to work for a company that respects its workers and humanity in general? One public relations professional, when asked about the type of client he would *not* accept, always answered this question by saying: "Let me put it this way. If a bunch of guys in brown shirts and swastika armbands came to my office and said, 'We're forming this new party and could use some publicity,' I'd show them the door. Beyond that, I stay open-minded."

Ultimately, the choice is yours. You're the only one who knows your tolerance for bullshit. You're the only one who can decide how much evil you're willing to stand. Short of breaking any laws, my mantra is: "We do what we have to do so we can do what we want to do." Even so, I have my limits.

If you're fortunate, you're not already a slave to your possessions and family obligations. You're not so financially overcommitted that your freedom is severely limited, increasing the odds that you'll have to accept whatever job you can get. If you want your kids to attend the best private schools, you've incurred a lot of debt, or your spouse/partner just lost their job, finding an employer whose values and vision align with yours may not be possible in the short term. You may have to accept that trade-off. But don't live in denial. Don't lie to yourself about the devil's bargain that you've made. Instead, commit to being the best version of yourself that you can be under less-than-ideal circumstances. Alternatively, maybe you can bucket the things you really *want* versus the things you really *need*. Maybe you can locate an opportunity to work someplace where you'll earn less money in exchange for greater happiness. Is that a trade-off you can live with?

There's a mental and emotional toll to pay for working for a company that's widely despised or that doesn't value anyone beyond its shareholders. I know this from firsthand experience. During the financial collapse that began in late 2008, I was working for AIG, one of the companies that triggered the disaster. In the months that followed, I had a target on my back. While commuting to and from Manhattan on the Long Island Railroad, I had to make a habit of tucking away the AIG ID badge that I normally wore on my belt for quick building access. If not, one or more of my fellow passengers was bound to stare menacingly at me before saying something like, "You guys are a bunch of fucking thieves." There were AIG executive assistants—people who had *zero* control over what had happened—who were spat on in the streets just because they were AIG employees. Some of these people had lost all their retirement savings. They were as much victims as the spitters, but do you think that mattered?

This is an example (albeit an extreme one) of the risks you incur by joining a company that's deemed evil. For this reason, and others, you need to seriously weigh the financial benefits of accepting a position with such a firm versus the potential drawbacks. Under the right circumstances, the adverse effects of seemingly intangible things like values, ethics, and social responsibility can take *very* tangible forms.

Draw a line that you won't cross under any circumstances. Is it working for the hedge fund that's ripping off little old ladies' retirement accounts? Is it the investment bank whose leaders delight in promoting a culture that pits one employee against another? Will the line move if you should ever lose your job? And in that case, would you accept a position with Cutthroat Corp. and agree to become complicit in promoting its values? Or would you accept the job but tell yourself, "I'll join Cutthroat Corp., but I'll rise above that kind of behavior. I'll work to make the place a little more tolerable for everyone."

Keep Learning about the Corporate Culture

Although preemployment reconnaissance can help you gather important clues to a company's culture, it will never reveal the whole picture. You have to *live* there. So, once you accept a position with a new company, it's important to quickly learn as much as possible about your new environment so you can formulate a plan on how to move forward. You mostly learn by *listening*—by taking mental notes during everyday interactions with fellow employees.

One way to learn what the hell's happening in a department is to make friends with the department head's executive assistant. Take them out for a cup of coffee and pick their brain. The "executive assistants" are the most powerful people in the office because they're the gatekeepers. I've gotten meetings with CEOs because I built a relationship with their assistant. Some people look down on admins, but that is a *big* mistake.

You can also learn from what you *don't* hear—from a *lack* of interaction.

When I was leading the Bank of America business process outsourcing account for Pitney Bowes, for example, my colleagues often competed to see who would take me home to enjoy a dinner with their families. By contrast, when I changed companies and the announcement about my hiring was made, not one person sent an email to welcome me aboard. Not one. Aside from my hiring manager, no one invited me out for coffee, a meal, or dinner. Now let's be clear, it was not an obligation of any one individual, nor was it wrong. It was simply an early warning sign that something was very "different" about the culture. Another indicator, which I observed in conversations with my peers: they rarely talked about their tenure with the company—for example, "I've been here ten years, twenty years." By contrast, when I later rejoined Citibank six months into the Covid-19 pandemic, tenure was frequently mentioned in conversations. Shortly after rejoining, one team member sent a note that read, "I've been here thirty-seven years. Let me know if there's anything that I can help you with. I know you've been here before, but the company's changed a lot." I received so many emails and calls like this that I quickly realized: (1) this was a company that embraced a level of change; and (2) it was very unlikely that my peers would knife me in the back at the first convenient opportunity.

There are as many corporate cultures as there are individuals and teams, and I don't pretend to be an expert. All I can speak to is my own experience working in a variety of cultures and microcultures. An organization may have one culture, but its various subdivisions may exhibit distinct microcultures. These include the following:

The customer/shareholder-centric culture. Everything in this culture is about the customer, the stock price, and the EBITA (earnings before interest, taxes, and amortization). Employees? Not so much. In this culture, you may be forced to do unpleasant things. For example, I was asked to cut the hours of my frontline employees. These customer-facing folks were sometimes verbally abused by customers and often asked by management to do more with less. I'd worked my way up from such an entry-level job to become a senior account executive. Tuition reimbursement and medical benefits had been essential, and I *hated* having to consider cutting these benefits for my subordinates—people who worked hard and had enabled my own success.

The collaborative culture. This culture embraces a one-team, one-culture, one-approach philosophy. The environment tends to be collegial and collaborative, resources are shared, and oneness is prized above all. There is no *I* in team here.

The consultant-driven culture. Consultants are running the asylum. The inventory of transformation projects is planned and, in many cases, led through the execution of the implementation phase and beyond by any number of consulting firms. In certain instances, an internal resource from the company is assigned to the initiative as a program lead to provide internal oversight and direction to the consultants. However, the reality is that this person is simply a figurehead, a resource to the consultants. To maintain your employment, and in some cases your sanity, it's important to understand how this happens. Initially, the consultants may have been brought in to provide industry-specific advice or skills that did not exist internally; in other cases, it's because of corporate politics or favoritism. The message may or may not cascade down from senior leadership that there will be an RFP (request for proposal) going out for a specific initiative. What you might not know is that the decision has already been made in private to bring in ABC Firm to lead the execution of Project X. The company is going through the RFP process simply to remain compliant with internal operating policies.

All too often, the A Team shows up to pitch their services, but then the B Team or even C Team shows up on Day One to kick off the project. Don't be surprised if the partners from consulting firms have card access to the senior executive floors or if they know more about certain areas of the organization than you do. The reason being is that some of these firms are on a retainer, and others have helped place former members of their firms at the most senior levels of corporate America. The running joke among my former colleagues is that, when we want to know what's going on in our company, we ask the consultants. **The cutthroat culture.** Achievement is the only thing that matters here. Hit your goals and get your bonus. If you have to cannibalize the business in one department to benefit your own department, so be it. So what if you have to lay off employees who have critical institutional knowledge to hit your short-term goals, knowing full well that you'll later have to hire replacements to meet the company's longer-term goals? And who cares if those new folks will cost more and won't be as effective as the laid-off employees, thanks to the massive learning curve? So what if you have to snuff out a colleague's candle for yours to shine brighter?

If you land in a cutthroat culture, Day One might resemble this gladiator-school scene from the film *Spartacus.*

SPARTACUS: What's your name?

DRABA: You don't want to know my name.

SPARTACUS: I don't want to know your name? Just a friendly question.

DRABA: Gladiators don't make friends. If we're ever matched in the arena together, I'll have to kill you.

I once worked at a financial services company that underwent a series of mergers and acquisitions, which combined the cultures of several companies. One acquisition was a well-known investment bank with an old-school cutthroat culture. Rather than firing the executives who'd become "redundant" after the acquisition, the leadership of the new division continued to follow a gladiator-school ethos. They would force the two people to fight each other for the remaining role by naming them "co-heads" of a department. Thereupon, each proceeded to make the other's life miserable until one of them quit. When the strategy succeeded, the division wouldn't have to pay severance to the departing employee.

Suffice it to say that when people are under intense pressure to hold onto their jobs, they can become pretty horrible human beings. Either that, or they will have what used to be called "a nervous breakdown." I remember getting into an elevator one day with a guy—a co-head—who began melting down before my eyes. Not a pretty sight.

If you find yourself in a cutthroat culture *after* accepting the new position, your options may be very limited. Aside from looking for ways to get the hell out of there, your only recourse may be trying to carve a small slice of heaven from the surrounding hell. In some cases, this consists of adapting to the new culture as best as possible without compromising your values, ethics, or sanity. In other cases, you may be able to change the culture a little at a time. But sometimes, the only good strategy is an exit strategy.

The corporate family/people-first culture. This is the antithesis of the cutthroat culture. Here, employees are appreciated, employee engagement scores actually matter, the benefits are generous, wages are fair, and you can expect to enjoy corporate awards, company outings, and sabbatical time.

Pitney Bowes under CEO Mike Critelli exemplified this people-first culture. The company was by no means perfect, but it was a darned good place to work. It had numerous mechanisms in place to recognize employees at all levels—from spot-awarded gasoline cards, free dinners, and movie tickets to quarterly weekend getaways (to destinations like San Francisco, Las Vegas, and Scottsdale, Arizona) for the top twenty high-performing account managers and their spouses.

Annually, not only were the company's high performers recognized with a trip to the annual PB1Conference (Pitney Bowes One Leadership Conference) in places like Hawaii, Bermuda, and Mexico, but the company also paid to bring your spouse, who received a gift basket upon arrival and certificates for spa time, daytime excursions, and spending money. Moreover, when you were presented with your award by the CEO, they would call both you and your spouse to the stage to receive the award.

Pitney recognized that the job could be a strain on relationships and believed that your spouse deserved to be honored and recognized as much as you did. I can tell you that my wife really appreciated this and really enjoyed meeting other spouses over the course of the four to five days, not to mention the entertainment by oldie-but-goodie performers such as Cyndi Lauper, Pat Benetar, Darius Rucker, and Kenny Loggins. Pitney provided a perfect opportunity for employee spouses to share in the success through celebrations and memorable experiences.

The friends and relatives culture. Just as I've worked in organizations where management helped employees become family, I've also been exposed to cultures that were—quite literally— composed of management's friends and family. I once visited a Texas office of the firm where I was working and discovered that it was staffed with the friends and blood relatives of the branch manager, who was also not shy about awarding vendor contracts to additional friends and family. I imagine that working in this culture is a bit like joining a mafia family, minus (maybe) the extortion and murder.

In addition to learning about the *organization's* culture to determine how (or whether) you want to move forward, it's important to recognize how your *own* cultural background can influence the views of bosses and colleagues toward you. This is especially true if you're an immigrant, a child of recent immigrants, or a member of an American subculture whose characteristics aren't well known (or appreciated) by the mainstream culture.

I've worked with people from South America, Japan, Africa, Korea, India, and elsewhere who were raised to do things differently from how most Americans do them. For example, a young woman who was originally from Asia worked with me here, but she grew up in Asia before coming to the United States to attend college. She was hyper-competent, but because she was raised in a culture in which it's often considered disrespectful (especially for women) to be assertive, she tended to be quiet during meetings. For that reason, she was sometimes viewed by her colleagues and bosses as "disinterested" or "disengaged." I had to remind my friend that it wasn't disrespectful for her to participate at meetings. I also had to advise her that some people would think she didn't care about the company unless she began to speak up.

If you come from a foreign culture or a distinct American subculture, I recommend that, during the interview process or on Day One, you have a conversation with your new manager about their working style. Ask questions like, "Are you open to me sharing my opinion?" Many managers will respond, "Yeah,

I certainly want your opinion, but there will be times when I don't have the option to hear it. I may tell you to table it." Others will say, "I'm a hands-on manager [i.e., a microman-ager]." In that case, ask them, "Would you like my insights on solutions?" or "Would you mind if I opine on ideas?" If the manager pauses and then says, "I need to give that some thought," leave it alone. If you don't hear a quick *yes*, leave it alone. But, in general, it never hurts to ask how assertive you should be in different situations.

Good people can land in a bad corporate culture, and the effects of that culture will manifest in the performance of the employees, the organization, or, in extreme cases, a courtroom. Years ago, I arrived at a decision point. I determined that, as a leader, I would gently nudge, politely push, and appropriately shove my organization toward high ideals relative to the culture, purpose, and values it publicly espoused. To accomplish this, I try to lead by example, model the right behaviors, and share social media posts that highlight the ethical successes at other companies. Other tactics include opting out of benefits that you believe aren't fair; respectfully challenging problematic behav-iors and situations; asking mentors, colleagues, or other trusted counselors for guidance; and soliciting advice from social media followers (without revealing any information that would violate corporate policies or rules).

The final option is to simply accept your lot, keep your head down, do what you must to accomplish what you came there to do, and then leave once you accomplish it. If you choose this path, that's okay, as long as you avoid causing collateral damage to the innocent.

Common Disappointments for Newbies

One big disappointment that you may experience on Day One is a lack of formal guidance on what you're supposed to be doing.

You're more likely to encounter this problem on reaching the ranks of middle or senior management. Earlier in your career, the roles tend to be pretty prescriptive—that is, the job descriptions are usually accurate indicators of what you'll be doing.

That can change when you're hired to manage people, processes, and products for a company seeking your unique insights, especially if the role is newly created. Here, your only "guidance" may be condolence statements such as, "We know this is new, but we don't have anyone with the experience to run this type of department." In short, you're expected to "hit the ground running" without knowing where the ground is. You've been hired for your industry or product expertise, with the understanding that you're not weighed down by the same old "idea baggage" as the in-house people. Unfortunately, you also don't have any in-house *knowledge* about how the place works, what resources are at your disposal, and how to successfully navigate the new environment.

Fortunately, the bigger the company, the more likely it is that you'll find people to help you (old friends and former colleagues) by scanning the corporate directory or visiting LinkedIn. "Great! So-and-so works here. I worked with her at ABC Co. Let me see if she can help." Start building an internal network to support your new role. Search for folks like this, and start engaging with them via email, social media, and in person. Send them a note that says, "We've been connected for a while, but I just joined your firm, so I'd love to pick your brain about how I can be successful at navigating this environment." Recruit friends, potential allies, and experts to provide you with the advice and guidance you'll need to succeed.

If you enter an organization as an executive, I also recommend you read Michael D. Watkins's book *The First 90 Days: Proven Strategies for Getting Up to Speed Faster and Smarter*. This will help you devise a plan for what to do in the absence of detailed guidance. In addition, don't be afraid to ask questions such as, "Are there meetings I need to attend? What should I expect to get out of this meeting versus that meeting? Are the attendees going to be looking to me for industry-related knowledge, or am I just there to listen? Of the folks attending this meeting, whom should I really pay attention to?" Start building a stakeholder matrix—what players do and why it's important—as well as the things you need to deliver for the firm and your manager(s).

By the way, don't assume that on Day One you'll receive clear guidance on what the deliverables are. Sometimes even the goals are ambiguous. It's as if your superiors have said: "We want you to go from New York to Savannah," and left it at that. Given this nebulous target, your next step must be gathering information to make the goal specific: "How do you want me to travel from New York to Savannah? Do you want me to fly, take a train, or drive? To what address should I drive, and what's the deadline?"

More often than not, the goal is relatively clear. It's the *means* to the goal that's left ambiguous, which is why you have to ask questions: "How do I do that here? What are the processes? Whom do I have to work with to get this done?" Sometimes, you won't receive satisfactory answers, and you'll have to visit the corporate job directory to search for people who can help you. Once you find them, don't hesitate to invite them out for lunch or coffee. "I just joined the company and would love to talk with you. You seem to be quite knowledgeable about A, B, and C, and I have some questions." Ninety-nine point nine percent of the time, these people will be happy to share their knowledge and insights.

If you're still early in your career, and you're unclear about how to proceed on Day One, ask your supervisor if a coworker can help. "Can I have an onboarding buddy—someone who'll be assigned to me to help me get acclimated? I need someone to answer questions and tell me what the process is for doing this or that."

Another common disappointment for newbies is discovering the "fine print" about their compensation, particularly their bonus potential. During the interviews, all they heard was 30 percent or 50 percent bonus potential—the key word being *potential*. So they accept the job and—whoops!—now they learn that the bonus isn't guaranteed. "I thought the bonus was certain?" Nope. The size of the bonus depends on hitting specific targets. . . . Read the fine print. However, what's not in the fine print is how well you fair during calibration sessions and what ranking you end up with relative to your peers (discussed later).

Another common disappointment can be avoided by recognizing, up front, that all organizations are fluid. Companies are forever changing. Many people don't realize that you can be hired one day, start the job, and within a couple of months or weeks, have a new boss. And your new boss is horrible. And your new coworkers are horrible. And they're not the people you interviewed with. It's like being put up for adoption.

I once interviewed for a position with a boss that I really liked. I accepted the job and was just learning the ropes when, six weeks later, some guy drops by my office to tell me that I've been reassigned and I have a new boss.

Some less common disappointments may include these:

- Learning just how unprofessional some of your peers and managers are
- Learning just how incompetent some of your peers and managers are
- Discovering that your unit contains one or more incompetent and unprofessional employees whom you can't fire for political reasons

The philosopher Heraclitus once said, "The only constant in life is change." That's as true today as it was in ancient Greece, so be prepared.

Finding Mentors and Executive Sponsors

I met John Vandenberg at Citigroup twenty-five years ago. He became a father figure, seeing something in me that I didn't see in myself. He showed me how to be a good executive.

When we met, I was a freelance commercial photographer sharing a three-thousand-square-foot photography studio in the Tribeca neighborhood of lower Manhattan. I worked the overnight shift at Citigroup for extra cash and benefits in support of my growing family. John used to arrive at the office early in the morning, around five or six o'clock. Early on he would initiate small talk, ask me about my professional interests and my family.

Then he began inviting me for coffee, to go get our shoes shined, and before I knew it, to meetings with senior executives. He'd say, "Look, I'm going to take you to this meeting, but I don't want you to say anything. Just grab a Redweld folder and put a newspaper in it to make it look like you've got some important papers. Don't ask any questions. If you've got a question, write it on a piece of paper, and slide it to me."

John taught me how to observe and listen. That's something a mentor does. Your mentor is your work coach, life coach, and spiritual advisor—a Yoda to your Luke Skywalker. As much as I learned about being a leader from John, I learned even more about the importance of striking the proper balance, while keeping family first.

The role of executive sponsor may overlap (a little) with that of mentor, but a sponsor is less advisor and more agent/manager—someone who locates opportunities for you, opens doors, and lobbies on your behalf.

At one point, my executive sponsor was a gentleman with whom I'd once worked at AIG, but who then moved to Citibank. One day, I contacted him and said, "I saw this inspiring speech of yours online. Can I get some coffee with you? I want to learn more." When we met for coffee, I shared with him that I had met an African American woman at a business meeting in our Los Angeles office who spoke fondly of him as an ally for underrepresented minorities and as a visionary leader. That's how I began building a relationship. The sponsorship relationship came later, after he invited me to his home in New Jersey to catch up, and we talked for a couple of hours. He kept asking, "What do you want to do? Do you want to go back to corporate America?

Do you want to continue consulting?" Long story short: He was aware of opportunities at Citibank, so upon deciding that I was interested in returning to the company, I called him: "Hey, Marcus, I'm thinking about going back." And he sponsored me. He made a few phone calls to senior executives and recruiters within Citibank and after a series of interviews—voila!—I was in.

That's how sponsorship works.

During your search for mentors and executive sponsors, keep an open mind regarding the type of person, or people, who might prove valuable for your career. In other words, try not to overlook potential allies.

For example, some of my most valuable relationships have been with executive search professionals and corporate recruiters. I recommend that you view every conversation with these professionals as a potential gateway to your next opportunity. Because they have selected *you* to present to their clients, it's quite possible they see something in you that many others don't. So, even when a placement effort doesn't work out, I maintain a cadence of touch points—quarterly or semiannually, by phone or by email—with recruiters.

In addition, after I established myself as an executive, I made a point of frequently inviting the search professionals and recruiters in my acquaintance to reach out to me for any future searches they may have, offering to leverage my professional network to assist them in finding the perfect candidate. Obviously, offering them something of value helps maintain and strengthen the relationship: "I have an expansive network of corporate executives at various levels and functional disciplines. Let me know if you need any help with anything. If you do, I'll refer some people, or you can call me and I'll give you a list of candidates who meet the requirements for the role."

The relationship can also be an invaluable asset for gauging the employment market at any given time. All you have to do is call your executive search friend to learn what a particular company is seeking in an employee and what the market is willing to pay.

Case Study: Sponsorship in the Making

Matt Kissner was the COO of Pitney Bowes when he visited that company's largest business process outsourcing account, the Bank of America, with a senior account executive. While he was there, he visited the support operations that I led for the investment banking division.

Kissner came into my tiny office to introduce himself, with the executive in tow. Not only did he ask how I was doing, he also asked what I thought Pitney could be doing better. I may have been a bit naive, but I felt obliged to speak truthfully. After all, this was a senior leader asking me a direct question. It never occurred to me to sugar-coat my response.

Instead, I drew from my experiences as a technical assistant at famous photographer Richard Avedon's studio, where the staff and celebrity subjects used to lunched together at a large picnic table in the kitchen. There, I had the experience of dining with the likes of Whitney Houston, Audrey Hepburn, Howie Long, Denzel Washington, Tom Hanks, and Donatella Versace. The famous and infamous dined, joked, and chatted in that kitchen before, during, and after some of the most famous photo shoots in history. It was there that Avedon would occasionally pull me into the conversations. (He had a penchant for making people feel special.)

"Curtiss," he'd say, "what are your thoughts?"

The first few times he asked that question, I replied by saying that I had no opinion to offer. Then, one night, studio manager Ling Li asked me why I kept quiet while everyone else was talking. I said that, compared with everyone else, I didn't have enough unique insights to offer. After all, I had been born in a small town in Georgia, grew up in St. Albans (a tiny section of Queens, New York), at the time had only one semester of college under my belt, and had never been outside the United States. "That's where you're wrong," Ling had said. "Dick asked you a question because he wanted to specifically hear your perspective."

So, in my office at Bank of America I told Kissner about a number of issues. These weren't the kind that would probably move the needle in the boardroom, but if he truly cared about his customers, he'd want to know how his customer-facing employees were doing.

I remember looking at the account executive's face while I was talking. He wore a look that said, "He doesn't need to know that." But I just kept talking. Soon, Kissner pulled up a chair. Then he gave me his card and asked for mine. Then he asked, "Do you like steaks?" I told him that I did, whereupon he said, "I'll have my assistant schedule lunch for us at Smith and Wollensky's steakhouse."

In the months that followed, I had lunch with Matt several times, and during those meetings he would ask about my career goals, as well as my opinions on certain senior executives. These were open-ended questions such as, "What do you think of so-and-so?" Nothing too probing. At our final lunch, he said, "I'm going to have the following executives contact you for one-to-one meetings. If you don't hear from each of them in the next week or so, let me know." Sure enough, within a week, I'd received either an email or a phone call from the assistants to these executives to schedule time with me.

The meetings were quite different and quite interesting. The executives' tones ranged from "What would you like to do in your career?" to "I'm not sure why Matt asked me to meet with you." The meeting that I found most disturbing was with the head of HR. When I told her the types of senior roles that I aspired to have one day, she rattled off an exhaustive list of requirements, many of which I didn't meet. (Some of the people who currently held those jobs didn't meet her requirements, either.) Did she do this to discourage me, or was she unilaterally "upping" the requirements for those roles?

Takeaways: Sometimes sponsors find you, so be ready for that moment. You never know what someone is looking for or what they will find intriguing about you. I believe it was my candor, naivete, and honesty that attracted Kissner to me. He was obviously seeking someone in middle management to tell him what he *needed* to hear, not what he *wanted* to hear. If I could relive this experience, I would ask why he expressed an interest in me that day. Knowing his reasons would help me to better advise young executives today.

Cautionary tale: Being identified by a sponsor does not guarantee the golden ticket, and others may continue to stand in the path of your success. Be wary of those who disapprove of your sponsorship.

The relationships you have with mentors and with sponsors should be very different. There are things you can say (or confess) to a mentor that you shouldn't broach with a sponsor. You can be incredibly vulnerable with a mentor, but a sponsor has to vouch for you, so you don't want a sponsor to start harboring doubts about your emotional fitness, capabilities, or ambitions. If I had doubts about continuing to climb the corporate ladder and was thinking of selling all my possessions and joining a Zen monastery, I might share these thoughts with a mentor. I would *not* share them with a sponsor. A sponsor has to vouch for me. They have to put their name and reputation on the line to advance my career. You don't want them to start second-guessing.

Sponsors allow you to leverage their social and political capital to advance your career goals. Mentors are a shoulder to lean on. A sponsor can do that as well, but some sponsors may not be your friend. You won't have a parent–child relationship. The relationship might be more distant and professional: "Keep me updated on your goals, and let me know if I can do any blocking and tackling for you." Sponsors are your voice in the room when you're not there. They aren't your psychologist or life coach.

I met Keith Wyche when I was a young executive at Pitney Bowes. He had recently been named U.S. President of Operations, responsible for fifteen thousand employees. I'll never forget the morning I saw the press release and looked him up on the internet to find out that he was Black. A number of us Black employees exchanged emails, phone calls, and text messages because someone who looked like us had finally broken through the glass ceiling.

A couple of months later I was in Dallas attending the company's annual leadership kickoff conference. Keith, along with a couple of other senior leaders, was sharing the stage with Olympic gold medal legend Bruce (now Caitlyn) Jenner, who was the keynote. Keith was charismatic and gave a very inspiring speech. Seeing him on that stage commanding an audience of that size was empowering and allowed me to remove the artificial limits that I had placed on myself relative to what the pinnacle of my career could be. The mentoring mantra of 100 Black Men of America, "What they see, is what they'll be," came to life.

A month later, I saw Keith at the company's conference center in the suburbs of Atlanta. I introduced myself as a leader on the Bank of America account, told him how inspired I was by his speech in Dallas, and asked him very directly if he would be my mentor. He replied, "It would be my pleasure," then gave me his card and invited me to the corporate HQ for lunch. That was the beginning of what has become a sixteen-year mutually beneficial relationship, one that has morphed from mentorship to sponsorship to friendship to brotherhood.

Finding the right sponsor or mentor is about building relationships based on respect, trust, and confidence. Once you earn trust and confidence, a relationship may evolve from a mentor-ship to a sponsorship because a sponsorship is something that is earned over time. But both types of relationship start when you reach out to a more experienced person. "Hi, I'm new to the organization, and I'm interested in blah, blah, blah. I see you run ABC Department, and I'd really like to get your advice on how I can navigate your division." From there, you maintain ongoing conversations with them. It's as simple as that.

When mentorships and sponsorships fail, it's usually because the relationships were imposed upon one (or both) parties by senior management—such as when the company suddenly decides that it needs a mentoring program and "voluntells" its executives to mentor junior employees. This is why mentorship and sponsorship relationships vary so widely in sincerity and effectiveness. It doesn't take an Einstein to recognize that a relationship foisted on two people is less likely to be productive than one the participants have organically grown for years.

Someone who's been "voluntold" may not give a crap. They may only be allowing you on their calendar for show—just to say "I have a mentee." Others may do it out of vanity or for self-promotion. I've had mentors who never did anything for me. They called me into their office for a mentoring session and spent the whole time taking phone calls. I once had a sponsor who was more concerned about my attire than what I could bring to the table as a leader. He felt that my tailored suits may cause my immediate manager to feel a bit insecure about himself. He may have had good intentions, but the relationship was a major disappointment.

Not everyone is cut out to be a mentor. Even if they have the desire, they may lack the right skills and temperament.

Can a mentor be an effective sponsor?

Yes. But not at the same time. The roles should be filled by two different people.

If I see a mentoring relationship moving toward sponsorship, I say to my mentee, "I'm going to get you another mentor because now I'm pushing you for jobs, and I believe the mentor and sponsor roles should be separate." This doesn't mean that the former mentee can't tap me for advice. It *does* mean that I no longer want them to "overshare." If I'm sponsoring someone for a job, there are some things I'm better off not knowing. For example, I'm better off not knowing that you're thinking of having seven kids—not when I'm considering you for a job that requires sixty hours a week of travel.

As your mentor, I care about you as a human being. I care about your spouse, children, and work–life balance. As your sponsor, I don't want to be put in the position of making important work–life balance decisions for you. "I'd love to recommend Dave for this job, but after hearing about his family planning ambitions, I really shouldn't. It would wreck his personal life." That's just one example of why you need a clear delineation between the roles of mentor and sponsor. Conflicts of interest can easily crop up.

Be Selective about Sharing Personal Information

Years ago, after one of my peers ("Candace") received an overseas promotion, I decided to hire her former executive assistant ("Chantelle"). Chantelle had been my executive assistant when I first joined the firm, and I liked her. She had an MBA, she was bright, and she accomplished everything I needed her to do. So I contacted HR to ask if Chantelle was available.

The next day, I got a call from Candace:

"Hi, Curtiss. Talking to you as a friend [she was never my friend], I wouldn't hire Chantelle."

"Why is that?" I asked.

"I don't know if she's focused on her work."

"What do you mean? Does she come in on time?"

"Yes. But she seems distracted."

"Does she deliver everything and meet her goals?"

"Yes. But she has a lot going on."

"Like what?"

"Well, she wrote a book," Candace said.

"Really? Tell me more."

"I heard she's been making guest appearances on television promoting it, and I don't know how she has time for that when there are things here that need to be done."

Candace had a lot of chutzpah. Here she was, suggesting that Chantelle couldn't focus on her job while writing a book in her spare time, when Candace herself co-owned a restaurant as well as a small chain of yoga studios. I thought, "Wow, you have some frigging nerve. You're lucky enough to have an executive assistant with an MBA who's been asked to go on television to speak about business strategy and finance. You should be bragging about how you hire the best and brightest. You should be picking her brain for ideas, or using your political capital to evangelize about her achievements beyond being your executive assistant, perhaps help get her a role as an advisor. We're in the financial services business, after all. Instead, you're weaponizing her success by bad-mouthing her behind her back in an effort to undermine a potential opportunity."

People will tell you to bring your "authentic self" to the work-place. I say, "Sounds good, but proceed with caution." Is your job, department, manager, peers, or company ready for that? As an African American executive, sharing too much about myself has sometimes come back to bite me:

- "How can you afford three kids in college at once?"
- "I saw that you made a big political donation to . . ."
- "You're a board member of 100 Black Men of America? What if I want to join?"
- "I saw online that you own an art gallery . . ."
- "He knows all these famous people. What the fuck is he doing working here?"
- "How does he have time for his family with all the work that we have here?"

Be selective about the personal information you share with colleagues and bosses. People *will* Google you. People *will* create "narratives" about who they *think* you are, what you deserve, and what you should be doing. It's important, therefore, that you prepare your own narrative to counter any preconceived notions. For one thing, your outside interests—like Chantelle's—might easily be perceived as conflicts of interest.

The biggest danger in revealing too much about yourself is that people will use those tidbits of information against you. I once made the mistake of telling too many people about my career as a fashion photographer with Richard Avedon. As a result, I received a lot of blowback of the "What the hell does he know about *this* business?" variety. (Many people struggle with the concept of transferable skills.)

Worse, some folks will share your narrative, with no corelating context, in rooms and spaces where you don't have a voice—places where nobody is coming to your defense. Next thing you know, an important decision has been made about your career, and you didn't even know that you were being discussed. "I don't think Jake would be good for this assignment. He's got five kids and won't want to travel" or "I heard Jake was going through a divorce, so it's not a good time. Let's give the job to [my best buddy]."

What should you do if people start prying? How can you hide parts of yourself without resorting to retorts like "None of your goddamn business!"

Change the topic. If there's something I don't want to talk about, I pivot by saying, "You know, it was a long time ago" or "I dabbled in that a little bit. By the way, how are your kids?" You can politely let people know that they shouldn't go there by changing the subject.

Don't ever let your guard down, no matter how innocuous the topic.

Years ago, I took my family to Italy for a vacation because (among other reasons) I got a great deal on the airfare. So we went to Italy and had a wonderful time. We visited the Amalfi coast, toured the Vatican, visited Florence, Tuscany, ate at great restaurants, and so forth. After returning to work, my boss said, "I heard you were on vacation for the last week and a half?"

"Yep."

"How was it?"

"It was good."

"Where did you go?"

I'm thinking, "Oh, no. He knows where I went because so-and-so already told him," so I say it out loud: "Italy."

"You took your whole family?"

"Yeah, the kids went." Now I'm thinking, "What's the relevance of *that* question?"

"Wow. You know, I'm Italian, and I've never been to Italy."

Now I knew what he was saying, which was, "How dare you go to Italy?!"

God is my witness, when it came time for my bonus that year, I didn't get it. I truly believed he screwed me out of my bonus because he was so envious about the Italian vacation.

Those of you raised to follow the Golden Rule may find it hard to believe that people can be so petty and vindictive. It may never occur to you that the boss would want to hurt you over something as trivial as your choice of a vacation destination.

Believe it.

There are people in this world who think that others should never have more of anything than they do. (This is particularly true, I'm sorry to say, of some people's attitudes toward African Americans. The Tulsa, Oklahoma, massacre of 1921, in which Black-owned businesses were burned and dozens of African Americans murdered, as well as the Wilmington, North Carolina Massacre of 1898, in which white mobs killed and injured hundreds while overthrowing the city's duly elected biracial government, are merely the most extreme examples of what can happen when jealousy is unleashed. More than once, I've heard Black executives talk about the "Black tax," meaning that African American executives are treated poorly compared with white executives.)

People don't need to know how much you spent on your house. They don't need to know that you have a second home or that your kids are going to good colleges. They don't need to know that you perform in a community theater. It's sad, but you don't want people counting your money and then deciding that Bob should get the bigger bonus because he needs the cash more than you do.

So, weigh the risks and rewards of disclosing personal information. Consider how you might come across in a Google search, especially if your social media profiles contain anything that could be construed as threatening—not because of anything illegal, immoral, or improper, but because of your fellow employees' insecurities or lack of self-fulfillment.

I'm not suggesting that you close your social media accounts and refuse to speak about anything but the weather. I am advising you to be careful about oversharing personal info.

Who the Hell Are These People?

On Day One, you'll be surrounded by a host of unfamiliar faces and personalities. Who the hell are these people, and what makes them tick? To answer these questions, I've listed some common corporate personality archetypes that you're likely to encounter.

Let's meet some of your new coworkers.

The Cultivator. Because Cultivators are adept at nurturing talent, they can be ideal mentors or executive sponsors. They like to provide encouragement and are good at spotting valuable skills and qualities in others. They enjoy offering advice and guidance and are willing to take the time to identify and invest in "diamonds in the rough." For the company, the benefit of having Cultivators onboard is that, by grooming in-house talent, these people help to improve the corporate DNA and reduce the cost of continually searching for external talent.

The Navigator. These people possess significant industry and institutional knowledge. They are well connected and have, as the name indicates, mastered the skills necessary for navigating various corporate environments. They know where the bodies are buried and who buried them. If you're unsure what to do, how to do it, or whether to do it, it's a good idea to consult a corporate Navigator. They can help you to efficiently direct your energies and avoid corporate landmines.

The Ambassador/Cheerleader/Evangelist. During my years at Pitney Bowes, I worked with a gentleman named Bob Mattis, who bled the company's colors for forty years. He grew up in a neighborhood that overlooked Pitney's headquarters and always dreamed of working for the company. After high school, that's exactly what he did, starting out in the factory and working his way up to senior corporate executive. He was proud of the company because of the opportunities it afforded him, and he would preach to every new employee about the firm's virtues. Unless you find yourself working for an extremely dysfunctional organization, you're going to meet people who fit this profile. They will work tirelessly to assimilate you into the culture. Resistance is futile (at least in their minds).

Captain Obvious. A person who makes a statement or statements of such obvious meaning or implication as to be entirely redundant, superfluous, or unnecessary. (Definition is directly from Google.) In fairness, this person maybe be stating the obvious because they really have nothing else to say but are fearful of giving a perception of not being engaged. The way around that without being Captain Obvious is by simply saying, "I concur with what's been said."

The Humanitarian. Another good candidate for a mentor or executive sponsor, a corporate Humanitarian who strives to make life more tolerable for their peers and subordinates, no matter how awful the company culture. They do this by never losing sight of their own humanity and that of other people. They maintain a healthy attitude and a strong belief that the welfare of the people belongs at the forefront of every critical business decision, even in the midst of chaos or when all hope seems lost. This is the person who asks, "How's your family doing?" before inquiring about the project that you're working on. This person cares about your complete self, supporting your efforts inside the corporate workspace as well as your outside interests.

The Noble Pioneer. These are executives who blaze a trail for others to follow. They take it upon themselves to do all of the blocking and tackling so that you can do your job more effectively. I have a framed description of this personality archetype in my office. It says:

Pioneers were originally soldiers employed to assist in the construction of field fortifications, camps, bridges and roads. Because they were deployed in advance of the settlers, they were seldom the people who got to enjoy the fruits of their labor. Instead, the strongest ones were sent forward again and again to conquer new territories. The work demanded both grit and might. Always looking ahead, the experienced yielded both wit and wisdom of the sort that can only be gained through the difficult work of opening up the next frontier. Seldom are the names of these men known by the legions of people who come later to settle, as if the road had always been there; as if the bridge had been a feature of nature; as if no personal sacrifice had been made in clearing away the bramble that would otherwise obscure the view for those who arrive generation after generation with hope in their hearts. Such is the plight and eminence of the noble pioneer.

Here's hoping you meet at least one Noble Pioneer at your new organization!

As you may have noticed, these personality types are pretty benign. To meet some of your less pleasant colleagues, see "Dealing with Asshole Colleagues" in the next chapter.

Remember, you are the captain of your vessel. Most of the ocean is smooth sailing, but never lose sight of the fact that there are sharks and icebergs in the water, so keep your eyes open and your head on a swivel at all times.

CHAPTER TWO

Never Let Them Kill Your Spirit

Your values is a disarray, prioritizin' horribly.
Unhappy with the riches cause you're piss poor morally
—Clifford TI Harris

M**any of us enter corporate America** believing it's a true meritocracy. We're told that if we gain admission to a good school and get good grades while pursuing the right academic degree, we'll land a good job. And if, after landing that job, we work hard, everything will fall into place. That's because hard work always pays off.

In my experience, this is far from true.

In actuality, we live in a world of perpetual tension between the ideal and the real. Although it's reasonable for employees, customers, and shareholders to expect alignment between the ideals of the organization and reality, people (and the companies they lead) can be unreasonable. More often than not, for example, promotions and bonuses are handed out on the basis of relationships, not job performance. (See "Employee Calibration Sessions" below.)

However, as long as you're aware of these things, and don't succumb to cynicism, you'll be well positioned to start aligning the ideal with the real—bit by bit—in your corner of the organization. In the process, you'll also be better positioned to advance your career elsewhere.

Employee Calibration Sessions

For those of you unfamiliar with employee calibration sessions, the first thing you should know is that—in theory—the objective of these calibrations is to evaluate and rank employee performance using a common standard. The second thing you should know is that, at some companies, the calibrations involve a lot of "horse trading." Prior to the sessions some managers cut deals with each other along the lines of "You support my employees, and I'll support yours." What's *not* said is this: You help me with my chosen employees, and I'll help you with yours, *regardless of how much—or how little—our favorites have accomplished.*

Although a number of companies claim not to use bell curves, this assertion is (to put it kindly) contrary to the facts. Once you go into the calibration sessions, you are usually working toward a standard distribution.

My advice is to brand yourself, promote the work you're doing, and explicitly highlight the wins. In a perfect world, your output would speak for itself. In *this* world, that doesn't always happen. Therefore, aside from your direct manager and one-up manager, the person best positioned to serve as your advocate is . . . you.

To back up that idea, I can't begin to count the number of times I've seen managers fail miserably during calibrations and roundtable discussions for reasons that include their own lack of engagement, lack of awareness, lack of commitment, lack of having a firm seat at the table, or fear of angering a more powerful or popular colleague. The most common reason managers fail to effectively endorse talented employees is a total inability to influence, negotiate, and advocate. This is unfortunate because leaders have an entire year to prepare for these sessions.

Your approach, as your own advocate or as a manager advocating for employees, should be the same (in principle) as for defending a thesis that you've written. After all, you—or the employees—are relying on *you* to tell the story. Your inability to do so can have a negative impact on your (or their) ability to obtain a raise, a bonus, or a promotion. In short, your advocacy will either help or hinder your (or their) career prospects and household finances. Think of your advocacy in these bottom-line terms so that you'll be fully committed to the process.

In a prior life, I participated in a calibration session in which the name of a young woman, who happened to be the darling of a parallel department, came up. She was presented as a 2— that is, a high performer—but was bumped down to a 3 on a scale of 1 to 5, with 5 being the lowest rating and 1 the highest. Not the end of the world, but there was an implied threat that another well-connected employee, who was submitted as a 4, would be swapping places with her. This threat caused executives to begin whispering in disbelief at the lack of support she was receiving from her one-up manager (who seemed distracted by his Blackberry). We all knew this young lady. She was an exceptional executive assistant and had just advanced to a project management role. A consummate team player, she was constantly working across projects, so we grew enraged when we realized that her one-up manager was unprepared for the session and was not about to come to her defense. Also disappointing was the fact that the human resources executive sat idle while all this was happening.

Ultimately, the one-up manager was embarrassed into taking action.

This is the sort of thing that routinely occurs in employee calibration sessions, and the average employee has no clue. They want to believe that the system works, that people have the best of intentions, and that their bosses will defend their performance, but that's not always true.

Therefore, I advise you to prep your manager throughout the course of the year by providing them with status updates, verbally and in writing. Your goals should be well aligned with the company strategy. If these goals are tied to some foundational work—building or managing something that enables a non-revenue-generating process or department—ask your manager what they would consider a successful year. Then ask what they would consider a home run or a grand slam. With this information in hand, you can develop metrics that will demonstrate not just how you met your goals but also how you exceeded them.

Please note that doing all of the aforementioned guarantees you absolutely nothing more than peace of mind that you covered your ass. Sadly, calibration sessions become popularity contests because there's rarely an opportunity to make an apples-to-apples comparison of individuals' work performances. There are simply too many variables to compare: resources provided to said employee, importance of the work being performed, and relative impact of each employee's performance. The goalpost can move to suit the needs of the decision makers regardless of how much you delivered over the course of the year. The conversation shifts from delivering all of your goals on time and under budget to the level of impact what you delivered had relative to your peer group. The issue is what metric is being used to make that determination, as well as the sheer lack of transparency in the process. So, where's the integrity?

In my experience, transformational work efforts around revenue generation and market share are always held in a higher regard than risk mitigation and foundational activities that serve as a bridge to enable growth—a mentality that I've always viewed as being short-sighted. Therefore, being good at navigating organizational politics and being known and, more importantly, well liked by the leaders in your calibration sessions will help you a great deal, so be sure to work toward that throughout the year.

Coping with Criticisms

You've been subjected to criticisms (fair and unfair) your whole life—from parents and relatives, friends and frenemies, teachers and professors. Once you enter the corporate world, however, the stakes are higher. Much higher. Whereas a poor high school report card might get you "grounded" by your parents, negative criticism from the boss might jeopardize your bonus, your promotion outlook, or your future with the organization.

Here are some criticisms you're likely to hear during the course of your career:

- You're not producing enough. Your work needs to be more impactful.
- You're not efficient enough/Your expenses are too high.
- You need to communicate more frequently, more clearly, and more effectively.
- You're not moving fast enough. Our competitors are out in front of us.
- The stakeholders are not happy.
- Employee engagement scores are low.
- Customer service scores are low.
- You're moving too fast/There are too many errors/We now have risk items.
- You're too friendly with your team.
- You run a loose environment.
- You're not performing well relative to your cohorts.
- Your presentation skills are not good.
- You may not fit into this culture. (This remark can sometimes mask racism.)
- Was there something wrong with your razor? (grooming/ appearance issues)
- You have an inability to manage conflict and tension.
- You're incapable of making tough decisions: you're a "pleaser," not an operator.
- You're not an extrovert, so you're not suited for leadership. (In many organizations, the people who *always* express

their opinions, no matter how inane, are often perceived as "natural-born" leaders.)

To protect yourself from *performance-based* criticisms, your first step should be to meet with your manager and, if necessary, other relevant stakeholders to review your portfolio of work. Here, everyone needs to agree on goals, timelines, and the specific outputs you're expected to deliver. Establish key risk and performance indicators, a key stakeholder matrix, and a reporting cadence for providing status and progress updates. You should also design a work and capacity plan to ensure you're properly resourced with adequate budgets, people, processes, technologies, and enabling entities (such as HR and Marketing support) to fulfill your commitments. By getting these agreements, you establish what, how, and by when you're supposed to deliver. This makes it much easier to manage expectations because you now have a framework that enables accountability. The framework also provides guardrails against scope creep and removes any ambiguity relative to what your bosses have a right to expect. Finally, you'll also have a mechanism to communicate concerns and escalate issues when blocking and tackling are required.

While you're doing this, continue to build your network of allies at all levels: subordinates, peers, and senior executives.

When it comes to communication, too much is usually better than too little. Overcommunicate what you're doing (unless you're becoming a major nuisance) so that your team and stakeholders are always in the loop.

In addition, leverage skip-level meetings—meetings in which you confer one-on-one with a manager who manages your manager. Your goal is to shine a spotlight on your portfolio of work *and* get to know the people who operate a level above your boss. The purpose of using these tools is to create and drive the narrative instead of allowing the narrative to be created *for* you. This way, if an unjustified criticism is ever made, you now have counterweights in place that can mitigate your need to personally respond. You'll have allies in the room when you're not present.

However, if the criticisms are valid, address them quickly. Create a performance improvement plan and communicate it to the affected parties. Let them know what you plan to do and by when. Once the plan has been executed, follow up to let the parties know that the issues have been resolved.

The following are key elements of an employee performance improvement plan. (Be sure to clearly list observations, prior discussions, and/or counseling):

- **Improvement goals:** These goals should be related to the areas of concern.
- **Activity goals:** A list of the activities designed to help you reach each goal.
- **Resources:** A list of resources to help you complete the improvement activities.
- **Expectations:** A list (or summary) of the performance standards that must be met to demonstrate progress toward every improvement goal.
- **Progress checkpoints:** A schedule of checkpoints for evaluating your progress with the improvement activities.

- **Follow-up updates:** A schedule of feedback on your progress.
- **Timeline:** A schedule for improvement, consequences, and expectations.
- **Signatures:**
  - Employee
  - Manager
  - HR representative (if a final warning is issued)

Here's what *not* do in response to criticism:

- **Don't** respond in anger.
- **Don't** react in an overly defensive manner.
- **Don't** respond without acquiring a good understanding of the facts. Collect those facts, understand those facts, and then stick to those facts if and when you decide to reply. If you're in the wrong, own it, and be prepared to share how you're going to rectify the issue, and by when: "I'm working with the team to better understand what went wrong and how we can correct it. I'll share my corrective action plan with you in [15/30/45] days [depending on the complexity of the issue]."
- **Don't** shift blame onto a colleague or a subordinate. Be confident when you're in the right, and be humble when you're in the wrong. Let the facts argue your case in the form of supporting documentation—for example, meeting minutes, service level agreements, performance goals and correlating reviews, status reports, and emails. This kind of documentation should be ever present within your overall

management structure. This applies even if you don't oversee any employees because you still manage situations, your career, and various other relationships.

Will there be times when the best response to criticism is no response?

Yes.

You don't always have to respond. It depends on who's doing the criticizing—your manager, a valued customer, a high-profile stakeholder, a member of your staff, a peer, or someone whose work or deliverables are highly dependent on your efforts.

As my career progressed, I realized how important it was to understand my stakeholders and to formulate a strategy and disciplines around how I managed them. (One important tool is a stakeholder matrix. Search out examples online.) Some employees are needier than others, and some managers are more hands-on than others. Some customers will never be heard from unless they have a complaint, so when things are quiet, they're probably happy. In reality, there is no cookie-cutter approach to managing criticism. A stakeholder matrix will give you a dashboard that tells you which people require more hands-on attention or extra communication. It reveals who complains most often, who has the most influence, and so forth. Leverage this tool—and your gut—to better understand if, how, or when to respond to criticism.

Beyond learning how to handle criticism, it's also imperative that you develop the ability to discern legitimate criticism from noise. Depending on your level, I strongly advise you to *not* respond to noise. Doing so is enervating and often counterproductive. Also, depending on how long you've been in your current role, you may not be entitled to the benefit of the doubt. Because bad news travels faster than good news, carefully assess each situation and the potential risk before deciding whether to respond. Be strategic rather than impulsive. The former approach may result in the occasional "lost battle," but you're more likely to win the war.

Case in point:

"Alex" was a bigwig at a company where I once worked. After an announcement was made about my promotion, he took the liberty of commenting on it during a meeting with his subordinates. "I'm not sure about that decision," he said. "Curtiss doesn't know the role, and I'm probably going to end up having to teach him. The decision seems very suspect, but, whatever . . ." Ironically, I learned about Alex's comments from one of my mentees, who happened to be in that meeting. (I say *ironically* because it was inappropriate of Alex to make the remarks in front of subordinates, but if he *hadn't*, I would never have learned about them.)

Alex ended up reporting to me. He possessed an incredible amount of subject matter expertise relative to the role I'd accepted, but he apparently didn't get the role because of leadership deficiencies, which were noted in his old performance reviews. Among other things, those reviews indicated that he tended to micromanage people and—surprise!—also had poor people skills. I treated him well because I needed him, and more importantly because that's simply who I am, and when he retired, I took him to dinner on my dime. There, I let slip that I was aware of the comments he'd once made. He explained that he'd been angry, bitter, and embarrassed because he was passed over for my job. He also admitted that he probably felt entitled, which was wrong. He closed by saying that I was the best manager he'd ever had, and he wished he'd had the opportunity to work under my leadership earlier in his career.

Managing the Review Process

Quarterly, semiannual, and annual reviews are the most important type of criticism that you'll receive. The equivalent of corporate report cards, they are often stored in human capital management (HCM) systems such as Workday, meaning they last forever. These report cards determine whether you're worthy of a promotion, a merit-based salary increase, bonuses, etcetera. Typically, each report also assigns you a "rating" using an aggregate numerical score that ranges from 1 to 5, with 1 being the optimal rating (an A+). Because annual reviews are also used by managers for internal hires, a negative rating can preclude you from advancing. Additionally, some companies still use bell curves, which means that a 3 rating keeps you employed, a 4 is a serious warning sign, and a 5 screams that you're in imminent danger of being unemployed.

Given the weight that many companies assign to reviews for measuring employee performance and effectiveness, it's important that you proactively manage the review process, rather than merely reacting to it. Toward this end, the first step is to establish your goals. These usually cascade down from managers, but to be of any real value, they must be SMART: **specific**, **measurable**, **achievable**, **relevant**, and **time-based** if they aren't already. Once you set the goals, have your manager review and approve them. If your manager doesn't schedule regular checkups to track your progress, you should schedule them. Once the manager accepts the tracking touchpoints, create a status report to memorialize the acceptance, and email the status report to them. If there are any success impediments, point them out as they occur and request engagement from the manager.

When it comes to managing reviews, your overriding objective is to make the process as *fact-based* as possible rather than subjective. However, depending on the company culture and events beyond your control, this is sometimes easier said than done. The most challenging environments are those that are tumultuous and fluid. Some examples include these:

- An organization undergoing a leadership change or being disrupted by external forces
- A management structure with ambiguous spans of control or scopes of responsibility
- An organization with a low maturity level regarding people/talent management

If you land in one of these environments, managing the review process will be far more challenging. Sometimes, it may even be impossible. In these environments, managers are more likely to generate reviews that employees perceive as subjective, unfair, and even arbitrary, potentially leading to arbitration or (in extreme cases) lawsuits. That said, you're far more likely to survive periodic reviews if you follow the strategies I've outlined and undertake a well-planned, well-documented effort to manage the process.

Dealing with Asshole Colleagues

If you work for a large enough organization, some of your colleagues *will* be assholes. They'll make your life unpleasant—even miserable—unless you learn how to deal with them.

Don't ignore them. Even if they don't *directly* make you miserable, it's important to be aware of their prominent traits and behaviors. To protect your career interests (and sanity), you need to familiarize yourself with the members of this species. To that end, below is a list of the asshole personality types that I've most frequently encountered.

The Shit Stirrer: This person's modus operandi is to point out problems and other negative issues and to make a bigger deal of them than they actually are. The Shit Stirrer will claim that this or that is "a mess," but will never propose a solution. Apparently, this personality simply enjoys the drama generated by injecting negativity into every discussion. Their behavior is the verbal equivalent of farting in an elevator and then complaining that the elevator stinks.

The Ice Prince/Princess: This member of the corporate aristocracy wants you to believe that their ascent to the senior executive realm had nothing to do with favors and personal relationships, though it almost certainly did—and they know it. Perhaps this is why their manner tends to be cold, aloof, and impersonal. It serves as a suit of armor that protects them from potentially uncomfortable interactions with those who know the truth. As a result, they will often pass you in the hallway or cafeteria without speaking, even though you're both on the same team.

Chief Bureaucrat: Sporting a wardrobe of red tape, Chief Bureaucrats will insist on convening a meeting of twenty people to make a decision that required only a quick phone call. They like to opine on matters beyond their span of control and scope of responsibilities, creating a delay in getting things done. By making life complicated, they help mask their inability to execute.

Mr. or Ms. Sky Is Falling: These managers catastrophize everything. Repent! The end of the world is nigh! After repeatedly failing to predict one apocalypse after another, you'd think these would-be prophets of doom would learn their lesson, but it never happens. Doing that would eliminate their self-styled raison d'être in the corporate culture.

Ambiguous Austin: What is this person's role and why are they here? Nobody seems to know, and neither do they. But like Waldo, they appear at every meeting, or they're always being spotted around the building, provided you look hard enough.

The Snitch: The name says it all. This person likes to snitch on people in the hope that it will advance their own career. If I suspect that I'm talking with a Snitch, I float a lie/assumption to see what, if anything, comes back to me. This helps me determine whether to trust them. This technique has never failed me.

The Bullshit Artist: "I'm here for you. I'm trying to help you. This will benefit you and your department/team." In reality, Bullshit Artists are totally self-interested. Fortunately, if you have any experience or knowledge of con artists, it's easy to spot these types. Their overly earnest "altruism" is usually a dead giveaway. As a rule, people who genuinely want to help will simply help—they won't give you a ten-minute "hard sell" about how badly they want to help or why something that's obviously detrimental to your interests is actually a good thing like Bullshit Artists will.

The Cult Member: This employee has been with the firm for twenty-five, thirty, or even forty years. "You'll have to drag me out of here kicking and screaming. I'm never leaving. This is all I know, and all I want to know. I plan to spend my whole career here," which is not a problem if that works for them. The problem arises when they take the "I'll do anything—good, bad, or indifferent—to make that a reality." At that point you're dealing with a cult mindset, so be careful not to say anything about the company that could be interpreted as negative. Because their identities are so closely tied to the organization and its reputation (the company is their whole life, remember?), a perceived insult to the company is an insult to them.

The Anointed One: This person lives a charmed life. They keep getting promoted, even though their job performance and/or academic pedigree is subpar. This causes everyone else to wonder, "Who the fuck does he/she know?" Unlike the Ice Prince or Princess, however, the Anointed One is often friendly and devil-may-care. They don't worry that their promotions, salary raises, and bonuses were not awarded on merit, and they don't worry what other people think. These entitled assholes only care that the good times keep rolling.

The User: These are the leaders who leverage their social and political capital—and the bandwidth of their direct reports, peers, and third-party partners—to advance their careers or personal agendas, without ever giving appropriate credit. They climb the ladder and leave their employees behind. You may not know it, but if you work for a User, much of your time will be devoted to making this person look good in the eyes of their superiors. It's like working for a politician who's perpetually campaigning for a higher and higher office.

The Opportunist: You never see or hear from these people until they need something. Once you provide what they need, they'll fade into the landscape—until the next time they need a favor. You can try asking *them* for favors, but don't expect a positive reply. They'll be too swamped with work should you ever need their help.

The Kool-Aid Drinker: If you show them the way through the maze, they will view you as a conspiracy theorist. They can't see the forest for the trees because they don't want to. They are scared of the truth. They buy into every excuse offered by leadership, no matter how ridiculous it may be or how poorly supported by the company's track record. I once had to plead with a mentee to stop posting glowing reviews of his company's commitment to diversity because it contradicted the reality of what he and his colleagues were experiencing and was misleading the masses on LinkedIn.

The Alpha Male: This macho man lacks emotional intelligence and seems to enjoy using foul language in the corporate boardroom. He functions like a bull in a china shop, maintaining a "my way or the highway" attitude and refusing to acknowledge when he is wrong, despite overwhelming evidence to the contrary.

The Rolling Stone: Rolling Stones aren't interested in the health of the organization. They are economic mercenaries who are all about enriching themselves and their cronies. They make their money and leave for the next opportunity before any shit hits the fan. I once had a manager who jumped from one senior role to the next every one or two years. Thanks to her incredible connections, she would land a new position, award contracts and high-level jobs to her friends, and then jet off to another company before senior management could ask her to leave. When I examined her career, I discovered that she had changed jobs seven times in the course of twelve years. Each job was either a lateral move or higher, making me wonder why, given her track record, new employers continued to hire her. Supporting your career and developing others are not priorities for the Rolling Stone because they aren't there for you and your peers. They are all about themselves. Unfortunately, your association with them can damage your career because you are now linked to them and their legacy of failure. They are a threat to the culture, and their actions can have a long-term effect on the stability of the organization.

The Company Robot: Because they display a lack of autonomy, Company Robots appear to have been programmed to respond to commands, but not to make independent decisions. This person has totally bought into the corporate culture. They struggle with independent thinking because they indulge in organizational groupthink and subscribe to a rinse-and-repeat mindset. You'll often hear them explain failures by saying, "Well, this is how we've always done things here."

The Email Warrior: This is the employee who is unsure of how to effectively communicate or show value in their role. Thus, they consistently send a bombardment of emails late at night, or very early off hours, with circular information to give the illusion that they are hard at work.

Note: Some people conform to just one archetype, whereas others merely lean toward one archetype or display the characteristics of multiple types, for example, a Snitch who also stirs shit.

If you find yourself in an environment in which assholes dominate, you have two choices: (1) minimize the time you spend in that environment; or (2) if that's not possible, because the assholes have been given dominion over your business unit, department, or branch office, look for a role in a different department, or even another company. If a malignant asshole has been given stewardship over the organization, you might want to investigate why the senior leadership has allowed this and whether they, too, might be assholes. Are there no employee feedback opportunities? Are employees afraid of retribution if they speak out?

There was a time in my corporate career when I took a lot of abuse from assholes in the form of covert and overt racism. I ended up on ulcer medicine at a young age. Leaving work without my dignity because I allowed people to talk to me (as my mother would say) "any ole kind of way," I got to the point where I was going to address it head-on because leadership allowed a department caste system and race culture to manifest where people of color in support departments (whites to a lesser degree) did not have to be respected. You were going to regret raising your voice at me. The turn-the-other-cheek philosophy was out the window.

MSNBC host Joy Reid recently posted something on her TikTok account about taking the moral high ground. But one gentleman responded that he instead subscribed to the "when they go low, I going even lower . . . I'm going to be an ant, I'm going to hell . . . to the earth's crust" philosophy. Although I don't agree with that, I've certainly been in situations when I felt it wielded against me. I believe they were doing this because there was little to no risk of retaliation—I take pride in being a decent human being. Even if I did think to respond in kind, in a corporate culture corrupted by assholes the response would have been reviewed and punished even more harshly.

So, when dealing with some of these people, my advice is to "keep your friends close and your enemies closer." *Don't* overtly shun them (in some cases, that's not even an option), but *do* understand what their motivations are and how they operate. Just as important, know your tolerance. That way, you'll be able to politely disengage from a conversation with an asshole before you reach your breaking point and say or do something you'll later regret. Keep your cool, identify the type of asshole you're dealing with, and determine how much bullshit you can stand before you'll need to make an excuse to flee their presence.

In the New York State Police Academy a zillion years ago, I learned the expression CYA: Cover Your Ass. Make this your mantra vis-à-vis assholes. Never let your guard down around these people. When someone has a track record of behaving like an asshole, thereby showing you who they really are, you'd be foolish not to respond accordingly.

Working in a toxic environment can weigh heavily on your mental state. Who wants to deal with that for a third of their life? This is why you should conduct your due diligence (see Chapter 1) before accepting a role, and why you should continually refresh your contingency plans so you can escape the madness if necessary.

Alternatively, you could try to mitigate the damage done by the assholes. For example, I try to model good behavior as a corporate executive, an entrepreneur, and a community leader. If I'm in an environment in which an asshole is given free rein, I do my damnedest to model behavior that is the antithesis of their behavior. One thing that I often do is invite members of other teams to participate in my team's brown bag sessions or "Coffee with Curtiss" conversations to discuss career development options and strategies. In this small way, I try to counteract the negative impacts that the assholes are having on the organization.

Overcoming Incompetent Leadership

There are as many varieties of incompetent leader as there are assholes, but in my experience, all of the incompetent subspecies fall into one of two "genera": the hands-on leader (*micromanager*) and the hands-off (*disengaged*) leader.

The **micromanager** either is temperamentally incapable of delegating or is willing to delegate *only* when they can lean over your shoulder to bark orders. (They want to ensure that you do everything in exactly the way that they would do it.) Typically, micromanagers aren't bad people. Many "grew up" in an environment where micromanaging was the norm, and they don't know any other way of working. Others are so insecure that they don't trust anyone else to do the job correctly. A friend once worked for a firm whose president shoved her hand into every "pie" that her employees were responsible for. As a result, the woman worked fourteen- to sixteen-hour days, six to seven days a week, while ingesting a growing list of pharmaceuticals in an effort to avoid a mental and physical collapse.

By contrast, the motivations of **disengaged leaders** tend to be more varied. For example, the wife of a friend once worked at an insurance company whose leader had basically retired without bothering to tell the staff. Delegation was not the issue here. The boss had so little interest left in the day-to-day "hassles" of managing the company and interacting with stakeholders that many lower-level employees were doing her job without any supervision—and shouldering the blame when things went wrong (which happened often).

Another friend worked at a law firm whose senior partner decided that, after ten years as a practicing attorney, he'd "paid his dues" and henceforth would focus on nothing but new business development. Soon, this guy had gotten into the nasty habit of promising the moon to prospective clients, leaving the associates with the daunting task of trying to figure out how to deliver.

Other incompetents are too busy playing politics to dirty their hands with fulfilling their responsibilities, while still others are assholes (like the Anointed One) who have been promoted well beyond their level of competence. They have no idea how to actually do their jobs and so they don't even bother to try.

Why is it important to determine whether a leader is incompetent and, if so, what type of incompetent leader the person is? By definition, a leader is supposed to inspire and to provide guidance and direction. The words *leader* and *incompetent* should never appear in the same sentence. Leaders have an incredible amount of responsibility, and in my opinion, their behavior should serve as a model for the behavior of those they serve. So when leaders are also incompetent, they do a huge disservice to the organization and its stakeholders, including you.

At some level (conscious or unconscious), incompetent managers *know* that they aren't up to the job. For that reason, they tend to be pretty defensive about any perceived slight to their authority and competence. To protect yourself from their fragile egos, you will need to monitor, review, and manage *them*, and establish guardrails. (Either that, or you can get the hell out of there.)

Incompetents may be very nice. You may genuinely like them. But if you let your guard down, their incompetence can manifest quickly and unexpectedly. Before you know it, you've been thrown under a bus. So, regardless of the formal reporting relationship, you should manage every situation that involves them. Whatever you do, don't simply follow orders blindly and thereby allow them to mismanage you into a detrimental situation where you've become the designated "fall guy." (If need be, consult with your previous managers on how to handle the situation.) If you're dealing with a micromanager, try to determine why they behave this way. Are they just the anxious type? If so, you might address that issue by overcommunicating. Do they lack trust in your abilities? Again, overcommunicating your progress may be the best solution.

I used to report to a manager who met the textbook definition of "nonconfrontational." His go-to response to matters requiring his attention, especially in the areas of problem management and corrective action plans, was avoidance. One day, I approached him, saying: "I know you're really concerned with several strategic matters [he wasn't], but I have a good relationship with the following individuals [all stakeholders who were a level or two above me]. I can take these things off your plate and represent you in certain meetings or manage certain areas [that caused him discomfort]." He gave me the green light.

By doing this, I acquired more senior-level responsibility, gained exposure, and built a reputation as a problem solver.

The silver lining to this dark cloud of ineptitude is that you can treat negative leadership experiences as learning opportunities—opportunities for observing what *not* to do. Some of the lessons I've learned include the following:

- The perils of overpromising, and underdelivering
- How a disengaged leadership style can contribute to a culture of mistrust and cutthroat behavior
- How surrounding yourself with "yes people" and "ass kissers" stifles professional growth and learning (That's because "yes people" and "ass kissers" will never tell you that you're wrong, even when you don't know what you're doing. Hence, nobody will ever do the emperor the favor of telling him that he has no clothes.)

We learn from excellence and we learn from failures. There's a famous quotation attributed to Carol Buchner and Maya Angelou that states: "They may forget what you said, but they will never forget how you made them feel." I strongly agree with that sentiment. I've had managers who were incredibly inspiring and supportive. They made me feel that I could accomplish anything. I've also had managers who were unsupportive and uncaring—people who told me that my career aspirations were too lofty. They reminded me of my first week of college when my academic advisor told me that I'd never graduate and should consider going to a trade school or getting a union job. Thanks to this advice, my confidence plummeted and I began questioning myself.

As a manager, I will never be the kind of person who tells employees about their limitations. I will be the manager who sees something in them that they haven't seen in themselves. I'll be the person who inspires them to strive for something greater.

Unfortunately, we are all just one incompetent manager away from hating our jobs.

Productivity Pressures

When you make it into a managerial position, you'll be expected to produce results. That's a perfectly reasonable expectation. What's perfectly *unreasonable*, however, is expecting you to achieve the equivalent of a manned Mars landing with a balsawood airplane powered by a rubber band. There will be times when your superiors will hand you such a "mission impossible" assignment. In response, your mission—should you choose to accept my advice—is to push back.

Typically, there should be a formal strategic planning process regarding the results you're expected to deliver. It's during this process that the work at hand is discussed, goals outlined, and resources allocated to deliver on the goals. If this process does not exist, schedule a less formal session to discuss, agree, and confirm all of the above—in writing. This is a negotiation process:

BOSS: I need you to deliver X by Y.

EMPLOYEE: Okay, I'll need A amount of this and B amount of that by ____.

BOSS: I think that's extreme. I can give you C by D, and we can check progress periodically. If the demand is justified, we can explore adding resources.

EMPLOYEE: Okay, so we agree on C and D, and we'll ring-fence the rest.

No one can rightfully shove unrealistic goals down your throat. Do *not* accept unreasonable or unrealistic non-SMART goals. Instead, use the kind of documentation mentioned earlier in this chapter to manage expectations or recalibrate the goals. Many environments are dynamic, and it would be naive to think that more demands won't be placed on you during the course of the year. However, if you're out of capacity, there's nothing you can do but go back to your boss and inform them that you need additional capacity to meet the additional demand. Either that, or ask them which items they want to prioritize. At the end of the day, everything can't be a priority, so don't put yourself at risk by failing to speak up just because your manager can't say no to their superior(s). A hard lesson that I've learned over the course of my career is that doing more with less is rarely rewarded.

I once had a manager ("William") who had comanagement responsibilities with another leader and was constantly telling the staff to push hard in certain areas. (His objective, I think, was to make the other comanager look bad by demonstrating that the staff wasn't meeting those goals.) If William wasn't hearing complaints about you, he would assume that you weren't doing your job. At that moment, I realized the type of person that I was reporting to and how alignment with him, or his way of working, could negatively impact my bonus and career.

At the time, the company used the bell curve rating system, manager roundtable sessions, and a relative forced rankings process. The same people that William was encouraging us to upset also happened to be the people who could make or break my career. Right then and there, I knew it was time to expedite my exit strategy. In the interim, I did my best to find win–win situations—areas where William and his peers had common ground—and I walked a tightrope to exploit What's in It for Me (WIIFM) scenarios for both parties.

Preparing for a Sudden, Unexpected Job Loss

How do you prepare for a sudden, unexpected job loss?

Regardless of how well you're performing, or how much you love your job and the company, *always* be open to conversations about new career opportunities. Remember: We're all one bad or incompetent manager away from hating our jobs. And given the amount of fluidity in many organizations, there's a decent chance that, at some point, you could end up detesting the place where you spend one-third of your life. Keep this in mind before dismissing an opportunity to at least *meet* with a headhunter or interview for a position with another firm.

Your social media, especially LinkedIn, should remain up to date. Your network of friends, allies, and supporters should remain strong, and your job-hunting strategy should be refreshed every so often. Reach out to key members of your network periodically, even if it's just to say hello or wish them a Happy New Year. Think of these exercises as a minor "must do," like changing the batteries in your smoke alarm.

Be consistent in nurturing your relationships. In other words, be sure to communicate with the people in your network every so often rather than simply growing your list of contacts by occasionally accepting a "please add me to your connections" request. If certain people are key to your job-hunting strategy, periodically engage with them in a non-stalker-like fashion. Do this by liking their posts (when you actually *do* like them) and by sometimes adding comments. Additionally, post items that position you as a thought leader or a subject matter expert in your field, and share posts that will encourage engagement, such as relevant white papers and business articles on topics of interest to the key players.

Believe it or not, I used to work with my own teams on their potential exit strategies, challenging them to develop a career pyramid from their current state through the end of their careers, with the understanding that nothing was etched in stone. They were merely being intentional and strategic about managing their careers.

I strongly encouraged members of my team to interview for roles that were posted internally. I recommended that they interview internally at least twice a year and externally at least twice a year. (I also explained that I was happy, as their manager, to provide career guidance if asked.)

Interviewing internally increases your exposure, helping you market yourself and create awareness about your desire to grow within the organization. If you're offered the role but don't really want it, politely decline. If you're not selected (and *did* want the job), all is not lost. Many times, leaders share great nonwinning candidates with colleagues so that they can be considered for other open positions or future roles. For example, I interviewed a young woman for a role in my organization and, although she was impressive, I didn't offer her the job. Instead, I recommended her to a colleague.

Interview externally so that you can stay abreast of what's expected of the winning candidates for the roles you've identified as stepping stones on your career pyramid.

In addition, upload your résumé to sites such as Indeed.com (but do this anonymously). Again, just because an employer requests an interview doesn't mean you have to accept.

One of my pet peeves (see the asshole list above) is when people contact me only when they need something. I'm not a fan of strictly transactional or superficial relationships. Therefore, every time I speak with a recruiter regarding a reference for a former employee or someone I sponsor, I use that conversation as an opportunity to expand my network with those on the front line of career progression. I share with them that I have a vast network and insist that they consider me a resource when they're looking to fill future roles. I check in with these folks at least three or four times a year, asking if there's anything I can help them with. That way . . . on the rare occasion when I want to ask a favor . . . they are much more likely to reciprocate.

Finally, it's absolutely crucial that you have a "rainy day" savings fund. Start building up this emergency fund when times are good so that you can leverage it during the tough times. Having a financial cushion will not only keep you afloat in the event of a sudden job loss, it can also prevent you from accepting a less-than-ideal position out of desperation.

The one certain thing about corporate life is that it's uncertain. Don't let this uncertainty rattle you. Embrace it.

I monitor the DOW and NASDAQ, attend the CEO's town halls, read the analysts' reports, review our customer service scores, and keep up with our employee engagement scores. I stay on top of how industry trends, emerging technologies, geopolitical forces, regulations, and so forth may affect my industry in general, and my company specifically. If you keep your ear to the ground like this, you'll dramatically reduce the odds of being blindsided by events that most people considered "unexpected" or "sudden." You'll see the handwriting on the wall in advance, and you'll be prepared with the equivalent of a career go bag to help ensure that you land on your feet quickly.

CHAPTER THREE

Establishing Your Identity

ike a product or service brand, your professional brand is largely a matter of creating and then fulfilling a certain set of expectations. That's your brand's promise. For example, if you successfully promote your brand as "master communicator," people will come to *rely* on that brand when they need someone to deliver a speech or presentation. If management needs someone to knock the socks off stakeholders via a PowerPoint presentation, who they gonna call? Brand X? Nope. They'll pick *you*—the go-to brand for all things communications.

When establishing a professional identity, the first thing to understand is that it's incredibly important to be true to yourself. Establishing an identity among an audience is not the same as *fabricating* one from whole cloth. The process is not about invention, but discovery—discovering and combining authentic parts of your personal identity to form a useful professional brand.

The second thing to understand is that life is about evolution. Therefore, your branding needs to be fluid, not fixed for eternity. If you're striving to thrive, you must accept that your mind and body are in a constant state of incremental change. Environments change, industries change, political leaders change, regulations change, moments in history change. Your identity may need to change with them.

For example: After the horrific murder of George Floyd, we reached a historical inflection point. Some companies moved from a hypocritical, passive, and superficial approach to diversity, inclusion, and racial equity to a more full-throttled approach in an effort to address past sins. Overnight, this prompted a host of organizations to modify their identities as they became more vocal about their beliefs in, and commitment to, diversity and inclusion, as well as racial and gender equity. Some of this rebranding is sincere, and some isn't. It's also possible that some of the "new" corporate activists now lending their voices to the cause may have previously been doing this work in stealth mode for fear of retaliation. Whatever their motivation, a lot of organizations have recently shifted their branding. Time is beginning to expose just how many were genuine champions of diversity and how many shamelessly used the tragedy to merely capitalize on what they saw as a momentary trend.

Generalist or Specialist?

One of your first branding decisions will be whether to present yourself as a *generalist* or a *specialist*. Although generalists are good at finding basic solutions, they typically can't tackle arcane challenges that require specialized subject matter expertise. This is the realm of the specialist, which is why every team should have at least one. While a generalist possesses the fundamental knowledge and skills needed to work across a variety of operational areas or functions within a business, a specialist narrowly focuses their considerable expertise in a particular area.

This doesn't mean that the generalist is a jack of all trades, master of none. Good generalists can work broadly *and* go relatively deep. They can't go as deep as the subject matter expert, but they have enough specialized knowledge and skill to know which questions to ask, as well as which specialists to call on when needed. In baseball, a generalist would be called a utility player. This member of the team isn't necessarily the best at any one position, but they're good enough to take the field as a short-term starter and can fill in at a number of different positions. Many managers find these players invaluable because they're so versatile. By contrast, the specialist is more like a designated hitter (in the American League) who specializes in home runs. This player is *the* go-to solution for a limited number of situations.

Whether you choose to be a generalist or a specialist, it's vital that you *choose*. If you don't choose this component of your identity, someone else will make the choice for you to fit their purposes. Years ago, for example, I became an expert in Six Sigma, a set of techniques and tools for quality control and process improvement. It was a popular "flavor of the month" during the late-1980s through the mid-2000s. I completed the training and then launched a black belt project at my place of employment to complete the certification process.

When I moved to another company, the COO sent out an announcement introducing me, which included a brief bio mentioning that I was a Six Sigma black belt. Because my new firm had low business process maturity, there were some who viewed me as a potential catalyst for change toward a more process-specific way of working. However, this expectation was never communicated to me by the executive search firm or my matrix of hiring managers. Nonetheless, the narrative very quickly took hold. I was there to drive change through Six Sigma, and I became known as the Six Sigma guy.

This narrative and branding did not benefit me. For one thing, the company merely flirted with Six Sigma. Thanks to a lack of commitment and discipline, it struggled to implement the methodology, which is why I often heard people say things such as, "I'm not sure why they brought you in. We tried Six Sigma, and it doesn't work here." Although the company could have leveraged my skills and experience as a general manager in a number of operations and functional areas, because of my Six Sigma branding, many executives viewed me as a specialist—a Six Sigma subject matter expert. Even worse, another narrative began circulating that I was not a good "people person," and thus unsuited to lead teams and drive business development. This was extremely far from the truth, but for a period of time, I was stuck with this branding.

This is one of the dangers that you, as a generalist, must be careful to avoid. If you don't construct a solid identity as a generalist, your bosses and peers may pigeonhole you as a specialist in some subject matter area that just happens to stick in their minds. Instead of being perceived as an excellent utility player, you'll end up becoming the equivalent of "Six Sigma guy."

Generalist or specialist? Which should you choose?

In my opinion, there's no right or wrong path to follow. It's truly an individual decision you have to make based on factors that include your industry/field, the company culture, and your career goals, personality, and tolerance levels. For example, in a company culture that is toxic and corrosive, you might want to be a specialist because this would give you more opportunities to work as an independent contributor (thus avoiding conflict). Or, if the organization's talent pool is not particularly "high caliber," you might want to become a specialist so you don't have to rely on support from a crew of underachievers.

If you're hoping to enjoy a long career as a specialist, be sure to stay abreast of developments in the field that support the digitization of the work environment, such as data science, data analytics, digital project management (Scrum and Agile), digital marketing, AI, and robotics, before choosing a specialty. You don't want to choose a field that's likely to be automated into extinction within a few years. Otherwise, the fate of many bank tellers, switch board operators, and travel agents could be yours. Take the long view and keep your eye on advances in the tech sectors.

I took the path of the generalist, though I *do* have relatively deep knowledge of certain specialties. As a photographer, I specialized in people (a broad category), though I also have experience with the people subcategories of celebrity portraits, fashion, and beauty. As a gallery owner, I focused on works of the African Diaspora (abstracts, portraits, photography, and sculpture). In my corporate life, I manage operations, which includes subcategories such as business process outsourcing, document management/enterprise content management, supply chains, project management/transformation, and operational risk.

As a generalist executive, I believe that I should have (at the very minimum) a solid baseline understanding of my industry, my company, our customers, our products, the markets that we serve, our history (because it has a way of repeating itself), our employees, and five to ten of our core business processes. This gives me a general working knowledge of my employer. I can then take this knowledge and drill down to specific areas of focus to find what's important to me and the company. This also allows me to determine whether my interests align with opportunities. In addition, it enables me to proactively identify situations that leadership either doesn't see or hasn't prioritized and position myself, or team members, for an opportunity to develop the brand and grow.

I can be something of a finance specialist, focusing on stock price, profit and loss (P&L), earnings before income, tax, and amortization (EBITA), return on equity (ROE), and return on investment (ROI), even without a deep understanding of the drivers. I also have a general understanding of people, processes, and technology. I can bring in subject matter experts to learn more about these areas, but knowing something about them enables me to ask more probing, drill-down types of questions before and after consulting with the specialists.

Is it important to broadcast to colleagues and bosses that you're a generalist or a specialist? It depends on what those bosses and colleagues value and whether that aligns with what you'd like to do. The key is *timing*. If the right opportunity presents itself, raise your hand high and scream loud. Broadcast to these people: "I'm here! I'm the right person for this opportunity!" In addition, during end-of-year performance reviews, be sure to stress how the role you played as either a generalist or a specialist benefited the company. Accentuate the positives! You want people to know that you're there and that you fit the brand you've chosen for yourself.

But be careful about presenting yourself as "limited." Tom Cruise specializes in action films, and to date, that has worked extremely well for him. However, an actor like Denzel Washington is respected because of his range. He can potentially work for as long as he wants, whereas I'm not sure how much longer we'll see Tom Cruise scaling skyscrapers and jumping out of helicopters.

Earlier in this section I referenced the phrase "jack of all trades, master of none." However, the complete original saying is: "A jack of all trades is a master of none, but oftentimes better than a master of one"—but again, that's for you to decide.

Take Advantage of Opportunities to Add New Tools to Your Box

If the last forty years of economic history have taught us anything, it's the importance of lifelong learning. Your job may depend on it, not to mention your ability to exploit opportunities for career and salary advancement. I'm not suggesting that you go back to school for another degree or professional certification. I *am* suggesting that you monitor existing and emerging technologies that might disrupt your industry and that you acquire new skills and knowledge to help you keep pace.

Don't run from change. Learn how to cope with it.

It's foolish to think that you can stop learning and still succeed. Success has a habit of bypassing those who stop adjusting to ever-changing realities. So, instead of hiding from the "change monster" or waiting for Superman to save you from it, find ways to leverage change to your benefit, whether advancements take place in artificial intelligence, robotics, data science, or Agile/ Scrum project methodologies.

There are plenty of lectures, free coursework, white papers, and open source classes at top universities such as Stanford and MIT to keep you current. At a minimum, teach yourself enough to engage in intelligent conversations about the trends and developments that may eventually impact you. The level of knowledge you gain will determine your level of engagement with these trends and developments, and that engagement may well determine whether you'll be crushed by the future or able to take advantage of it.

Some knowledge and skills may prove more valuable (and durable) than others, but even if you don't apply certain tools very often, the quest for personal and professional improvement is never a waste of time. That said, it *is* important to weigh the necessary investment of time, effort, and money for acquiring the new knowledge against how you plan to leverage the tools and market them to your bosses, stakeholders, or hiring managers. If peak fitness is your motivation for buying a Peloton bike, but you end up using it as a coat rack, that's a bad investment.

On the other hand, you may have reason to acquire tools that aren't exactly cutting edge—tools that aren't valuable to progressive organizations but that could benefit you in an organization that's slow to embrace change or in the midst of a transformation. In the latter case, the company may need certain legacy skills and knowledge to conduct an orderly transition to its desired future state.

Acquiring new skills is essential to your development as an employee, and as a person. You'll find that many new skills are transferable, so you can leverage them in your day-to-day work life as well as in outside endeavors. I view each continuous learning opportunity as a growth opportunity because it helps me achieve my professional goals and, more importantly, better positions me to teach and mentor.

Uncovering Your Abilities

Task-specific skills and knowledge aren't the only tools you should add to your box. You should also seek to identify personality traits, abilities, and talents that might benefit you, your colleagues, and the organization. Often, people who work closely with you will be the first to observe and point out these abilities. These are the strengths that people see in you, which you may not have seen in yourself (or recognized as strengths). For example, here are a few of my strengths that my managers identified over the years:

- Curtiss . . . demonstrated the very best of competencies of any business leader, consistently and repeatedly **finding and developing "diamond in the rough" talent**. I cannot speak highly enough of his leadership.
- I've always found him to be **honest, caring, and thoughtful**, all character traits that earned the respect of his employees, peers, and senior management.
- Another thing that makes Curtiss stand out is his **creative lens**. He **has the unique ability to see the potential where others see failure**, both in operations and more importantly in people, our most important asset.

Without third-party recognition of these abilities, I might never have viewed them as strengths. Until then, I considered these virtues as garden-variety values, the ones that my parents and grandparents had instilled in me: honesty, integrity, doing right by people, and trying to make a positive difference in the lives of others. It was only later in life that I learned that these "common" values are not that commonly practiced.

One of the best ways to uncover latent abilities is to carefully read your performance reviews and ask questions if you're not clear on what the author(s) meant. (In addition, be sure to analyze any 360-degree feedback surveys.) Another tactic is to (informally) ask your peers to identify what they believe to be your hidden "superpowers." Pay close attention to what they say, especially if the same observations keep cropping up from one person to the next.

A word of caution: Understand the maturity of your environment. Know the difference between a well-intended initiative designed to effectuate positive change and a check-the-box exercise. Be very careful with providing 360-degree feedback when it's not totally positive. You can end up with a target on your back by your manager or a one-up manager simply because, as Jack Nicholson's character Col. Nathan Jessup in *A Few Good Men* would say, they "couldn't handle the truth," regardless of how diplomatically communicated.

Keep your ears open for traits and talents that could have the biggest impacts. If someone says, "We couldn't have done X without you," ask them to elaborate. Tell them you're trying to learn more about your strengths and weaknesses, and if there's anything you're doing especially well—things that really add value—you want to know about them so you can continue building on them.

Wole Coaxum, a Wall Street banking veteran, former colleague, and founder and CEO of MoCaFi, once told me that I had great people management skills. He said I presented myself in a way that people valued because they saw honesty and integrity. As a result, people generally trusted me. In addition to this feedback, he encouraged me to join the wealth management program, saying, "I would trust you with *my* money because you're hardworking and competent."

At the time, I was a manager in investment banking support services, an operations role, but his assessment empowered me to believe that anything was possible. Thanks to his observations about me, I *consciously* recognized that I was good at stakeholder management because I had a strong ability to manage customer relationships.

With this in mind, I used these talents in my next role (at Pitney Bowes) as an account manager for a business process outsourcing relationship with a company that eventually became our biggest customer: the Bank of America. I built strong relationships with the bank's managers in supply chain and investment banking, and quickly moved up from senior manager to area manager to regional director to general manager. This last role required heavy stakeholder management and business development, for example, selling solutions and services without being too explicit about it, and relationship building. None of this would have happened if I hadn't received—and *listened to*—those earlier comments about my people skills.

While conducting your search for hidden abilities and talents, don't overlook the weaknesses that you also uncover. Ultimately, your objective is to enhance your strengths and shore up the weaknesses. For example, although it took time, I came to recognize that one of my biggest weaknesses was unfettered optimism. Until then, I usually ascribed only the best intentions to other people's behavior, but I eventually recognized that this belief was a weakness—one that was both naive and irresponsible. At the end of the day, trust should be earned, not handed out like Halloween candy to anyone who happens to ring your doorbell. Slowly (and sometimes painfully), I realized that people have different motives. It's entirely possible that members of a group will subscribe to the same goal for very different reasons and take very different paths toward the goal, some noble, some not so noble. To shore up my weakness, I constructed a bullshit detector that now operates around the clock, scanning the vicinity for those who are determined to do the right thing and those intent on doing the wrong thing. Thanks to this, I also do a much better job today of analyzing situations, their root causes, and making comparisons based on industry best practices.

How much effort should you devote to shoring up weaknesses versus enhancing your strengths?

It depends on how wide the gap is between what's required to deliver in your role and the current state of your abilities. For example, if your biggest weakness is delivering PowerPoint presentations, and you work at Amazon, this weakness is irrelevant because Amazon doesn't use PowerPoint. On the other hand, if you work for a management consultancy, this weakness is something you'd better shore up in a hurry.

In sum, deciding which strengths and weaknesses need work depends, in large part, on your particular industry, company, department. and role. If you're looking to grow within a specific role or organization, discover which strengths your manager or the organization values most, and then work to develop and amplify them.

At some point, however, the law of diminishing returns is bound to kick in. You'll be enduring too much pain for too little gain. Once you reach that point, it will no longer make sense to keep trying to enhance a particular strength or shore up a particular weakness. You'll know you've reached this threshold when: (a) perfect has become the enemy of good, or (b) it becomes clear that your self-improvement effort no longer provides value. In some cases, shoring up weaknesses won't even be necessary because your strengths offset the negative impact of the weaknesses.

Some additional tools to help you uncover your abilities include:

- YouTube lectures
- LinkedIn posts
- Analysis of your personality test results (such as the Myers-Briggs Type Indicator®)
- Analysis of maturity assessments
- Analysis of skills gap assessments

Ultimately, the best way to enhance strengths and shore up weaknesses is through real-world application of your skills and talents in an environment that provides ongoing feedback.

Managing Your Brand

Once you have consciously established your brand (as opposed to being pigeonholed with one), your brand is on display every day that you're out in the physical or virtual world. This affords you an endless supply of opportunities to enhance your brand . . . or damage it.

Regardless of who you are, what your role is, and what brand you've created, it's vital to manage and protect your brand—or brands. I have multiple brands that comprise who I ultimately am. One of these is *Mr. Fix-It*, the organizational turnaround expert who's always willing to take on the difficult assignments that other executives avoid. I subscribe to the "If I fail, it won't be due to lack of effort" philosophy.

I manage my brand by how I show up for every situation. I validate my brand through words, deeds, and actions . . . by walking the talk. I'm very conscious and intentional about the types of posts that I "like" on LinkedIn, the types of engagements I accept, and the types of boards on which I serve. I'm aware that each and every relationship that I have can either advance my brand or erode it.

Brand and image consultant David McKnight, a former employee, who later became a colleague and advisor, taught me to think of my brand in four dimensions. This is how I define my professional brands:

- **Thought leadership:** Operations excellence, diversity/ inclusion/racial equity
- **Actions:** Connector; investor in people, the arts, and community
- **How I make people feel:** Cared for, invested in; loans his humanity to his colleagues at all levels
- **Presence (visual/oral presentation):** Polished look and authentic speaker

Feel free to adopt this model and fill in the traits that apply to you. Whatever you do, don't peddle a false brand or a brand that you can't live up to. As long as you create an authentic brand and always walk the talk, the rest will fall into place. Nobody likes a phony, so create a brand that reflects your authentic self.

If your brand is tarnished or, worse, you're "assigned" an unappealing brand by others, all is not lost. It *is* possible to give your brand a makeover.

Early in my career, I managed a back-office digital print, graphics, and mail operation. During this time, I learned that people had begun referring to me as the "print guy." This was a major understatement regarding the scope of my expertise, which necessitated I oversee technology, data, design, project management, and shared services centers of excellence. To put it mildly, I was annoyed by the label "print guy" and realized that I needed to change the way I was perceived.

I wanted to be regarded as an operations executive or (in some scenarios) an enterprise content management executive—a much more impressive (and highly compensated) role than "print guy." To accomplish my rebranding, I began delegating more of my responsibilities, and in some cases authority, to subordinates. This freed me to spend more time interacting with senior leaders and external stakeholders so that I could position myself as a generalist who provided much more value than simply "printing."

Later in my career, I had to undertake yet another branding facelift. This time, I was perceived as an individual contributor, despite years of leading large-scale operations. Folks didn't think that I could scope a large project with a significant financial impact. Before I knew it, I'd been assigned a brand that I didn't deserve or want. I've since learned that when this happens—when others put you in a box of their choosing—it's up to *you* to rebrand yourself. You have to climb out of that box and find another one that better suits your aspirations.

At the time, many people viewed my operation as insignificant. To prove them wrong, I decided to crunch some numbers. I documented that the organization was tying up $500 million annually in areas that were managed in a fragmented way, but that I possessed the subject matter expertise to turn that around. I traveled around the world to conduct baseline assessments and leveraged regional CFOs in the United States, Europe, Middle East, and Africa (EMEA), Asia Pac, and Latin America to gain access to the financial data and country heads needed to sponsor my effort. The half-billion-dollar opportunity opened their eyes to my ability to size and scope an operation in a complex environment.

The takeaway is that *I had to find an opportunity for rebranding myself* in the form of a project that mattered to the higher-ups—a project that forced them to take notice of my abilities.

If you understand how others perceive you, you'll have a better understanding of your brand. If that brand is solid, well established, and well regarded, you'll win respect and get the benefit of the doubt. If your brand is misunderstood, or you've been stuffed into a box, don't accept it. Look for opportunities and *create* opportunities to give your brand a makeover.

Water the Seed, Not the Rock

A sower went out to sow his seed. And as he sowed, some fell along the path and was trampled underfoot, and the birds of the air devoured it. And some fell on the rock, and as it grew up, it withered away, because it had no moisture. And some fell among thorns, and the thorns grew up with it and choked it. And some fell into good soil and grew and yielded a hundredfold.

—Luke 8:4–8

Your energies and resources are precious. As such, you should focus them on areas that are important to you. For example, if human capital development is your passion, you could focus on mentoring an employee others have written off. (She's okay, but they can't see any upside in mentoring her.) *You*, on the other hand, may see an opportunity to learn something—from the perspective of a gardener, to gain a "green thumb" through the experience. Keep in mind that there's always a two-way development process in any human interaction, in this case, the gardener and the seed. The seed is the opportunity for growth through valuable experience, relationships, and actions that help you learn what to do, how to do it, and with whom. The seeds catapult you into a better future.

For most people, there's nothing worse than working in a dead-end job. However, maybe you don't care that a position offers no opportunities for promotion. Instead, you find it gratifying in other ways. Maybe you'd rather teach, improve processes, and drive other changes from your little corner of the organization.

Think about your career as a garden: with proper nurturing, seeds will turn into plants, but the rocks, well . . . the rocks will always be rocks.

Watering People

At some point in your career, you will work in a role that capitalizes on the traits of your authentic self and leverages your talents and leadership skills. Others may tap you as a mentor. Before you take on the job of mentoring, there are three key insights you should understand. First, you need to know the difference between a seed and a rock. Next, you need to understand how much water to apply to seeds, and then when to stop watering. And you must never lose sight of the fact that some rocks (like coal) have the potential to become precious gems. Distinguishing seeds and nascent gems from rocks requires a higher level of wisdom, knowledge, and discernment so that your efforts and wisdom are not wasted.

As a mentor, an advocate, and a sponsor, I take pride in seeing something in someone, something not obvious to others. I truly embrace the challenge of developing a rough diamond because it can be so rewarding, for both of us. It's disappointing, however, when some of the people who receive my investment come to believe that they are entirely self-made and then choose not to pay things forward. (That's a fourth key concept of mentoring: continuing the cycle of passing gifts of wisdom and advice onward to new recipients.) I believe that we all owe a debt of gratitude to someone, whether it's an individual or an entire community, for helping us become who we are.

Although everyone has the potential to change and flourish, not everyone will. And I accept that. With time, I've learned that it's important to understand what your mentees and other "students" want to achieve. (You can do this by asking them in a one-to-one session or, if you're working at a large organization, this information can be captured with strategically crafted survey questions.) It's great to offer people a view of the world and help them understand where they have the *potential* to fit in. However, we should avoid trying to shove the proverbial square peg into the round hole just because *we* think it would be a great fit.

Is it important for your friend, peer, or mentee to be a C-suite executive, make lots of money, and send their kids to boarding school? Or are they interested in a career that affords greater work–life balance, with plenty of time for helping the kids with homework, going to school plays, being a hands-on parent, and having the opportunity to spend quality time with their parents, who are advancing through the elder stages of life? Ask questions and find out. I'm proud—and my kids were happy—that I was able to strike enough balance to enjoy continuous career growth while still making my kids a priority. And I'm grateful to every leader who understood this and helped me achieve the goal rather than trying to tempt me onto a path that I would have regretted later.

Watering Operational Situations

I've developed a pretty sound reputation as a transformation expert—someone who possesses the ability to turn around underperforming departments, businesses, and projects. This requires discernment as well as connections to the historical context and the hidden stories behind the reports. Although the reports may state that a project underperformed because of poor execution, the untold story may tell a different tale—that the project is failing for several reasons, including underinvestment, behind-the-scenes politicking, or conflicts with the goals of a higher power inside the organization. By uncovering this information, I can make better decisions around how much water I want to use in a situation or simply whether to turn off the sprinkler.

One of my favorite quotes comes from Peter Drucker, who said, "You can't manage what you don't measure." Most of us are aware of this fact, yet some of the largest, most famous brands in the world go about their business in a haphazard way. They measure some things and ignore others. For example, Shawn Rochester, in his book *The Black Tax,* lays out an extraordinarily compelling case documenting the enormous financial cost of current and past anti-Black discrimination. He then establishes a framework that Black Americans and other concerned parties can use to eliminate this tax and create the six million jobs and 1.4 million businesses that are missing from the Black community. Again, if you don't care to measure it, you'll miss the opportunities that abound.

You may find yourself in a situation where you're constantly hitting your head against the ceiling. You're doing all of the right things, but the opportunities simply don't appear. In this case, you have to survey the situation and ask yourself if there's a realistic path forward within a timeframe that works for you. If the answer is no, save your water, and leave the firm. The company's leaders obviously don't believe in you, choose to ignore you, or won't acknowledge that they have a broken talent management system.

Pay attention to whom and where you are devoting your time, talent, and treasure, and track the investment and the return. It's the responsible thing to do. But keep in mind that sometimes the best thing you can do for a person or a situation is to stop making yourself available to them. Walk away. Your time must be respected. One of many things I've learned from my wise and virtuous wife is to have the courage to stop being overly accommodating by saying "no" more often. By doing this, my "yes" acquires more meaning and value.

If you're focusing your energies on the wrong area, or person, warning signs will pop up. One is a persistent lack of progress relative to the goals that you've set. Another is when the effort becomes overwhelming—a drain on your emotions, with no end in sight. When it comes to people, another warning sign is the feeling that you're being taken for granted, a distinct lack of respect or gratitude coming from your mentee, stakeholders, or customers. If the target audience doesn't respect what you're trying to do for them, it may be time to pull the plug.

Simply knowing who you are and what you stand for is incredibly empowering. It better enables you to move forward with a sense of confidence and purpose primarily because you know who you are—and who you're not—which is important for maintaining focus on the things that are mission critical to your career and life strategy. This in no way means that you stop evolving; you simply add the complementary elements as you grow and prioritize which parts you emphasize as you determine how you continue to show up in the future.

An Interview with Leadership Consultant and Executive Coach Verna Ford

Verna Ford is a leadership consultant, executive coach, and diversity and inclusion advisor. She also served as my executive coach for a year.

CJ: How do you know if you're successfully projecting your brand?

VF: Other people will confirm your brand in different ways. If you are a hard worker and a good worker and no one notices, then that means that you're a hard worker and a good worker, but a poor marketer. If you are very smart but difficult to work with, people will ask for your insights but will not invite you to be a member of the team. If you are risk-averse and waiting for others to make things happen on your behalf, you will likely wait a very long time.

If you are observant, there is plenty of evidence about how successfully you are projecting your brand.

CJ: If you determine that you're not projecting the brand you want, how do you correct people's perceptions of you?

VF: First, everything about you and your work must exemplify the brand you want to convey. Beyond that, you need an elevated skillset to promote your value. Most people are not thinking about your "brand." They care that the work gets done. You must tell decision makers how to think about the contributions you are making to the business. Again, you must learn the language, become unafraid to create awareness and appreciation for your capabilities, while remaining grounded, unpretentious, and approachable. If that seems like a tall order, you need an executive coach.

CJ: That brings me to my next question: At what point should someone engage an executive coach?

VF: Any time is a good time, but especially when you look around and things appear illogical. You are doing the work, but not seeing the career results you are looking for. You want to make something different happen, but you are not sure how to make it so. A coach can help you think through career strategies and help you understand how the culture of business really works.

It's also a good time when you're dealing with colleagues who understand that not everyone is going to be promoted, and they're willing to get dirty by undermining you, your work, or your confidence. Or when people making promotional decisions simply can't imagine you in an advanced role, so they look past you. A coach can help you negotiate what I call the politics of success.

A coach may ask you a series of questions—some may be very provocative—but the questions will be designed to help you think through your situation. A coach does not tell you what to do. You engage an executive coach because it's good to have someone help you think through the options.

Under some circumstances, you may be able to achieve the same goals by speaking to your manager, but there are two clear benefits of accessing a coach:

1. The only vested interest of a coach is to help you get what you want. A manager may feel

obligated to first protect their own interests. For example, keeping a great worker in position to ensure the team's quarterly numbers are met.

2. If the coach comes from outside your organization, you can also be better assured of confidentiality with respect to your more sensitive development needs and goals, such that they don't wind up as "weaknesses" in your next performance review.

CJ: What area the characteristics of executives whose jobs you are brought in to save?

VF: I have never had to coach an executive about their work ethic or technical ability. It was mostly about whether the employee was a good cultural fit or had strong workplace relationships. It was about them getting out of the weeds, moving into the world of strategy, and being able to communicate effectively at higher levels. The language you speak at a senior level is different from the language used in middle management. If you don't know the language, you will come off as too junior to hold certain positions.

I have a client who struggled with asking for what she wanted from the company. She was polite and deferential. She came across as a supplicant, begging for what she needed to do her job well. Now, she most often gets what she's after. It's a matter of fluency with "the language of business."

CJ: **What are the attributes of firms that have a true meritocratic culture?**

VF: Meritocracy is an ideal for an organization and its leaders to work toward. However, operationally, a true meritocracy depends on every leader being objective and fair with every employee, as measured against an explicit standard of excellence. Ask yourself, Have I ever been in a work situation where every leader does the right thing by each employee? It's a goal to strive for, and if companies hold executives accountable . . . they will have a better chance of achieving that goal. Unfortunately, most people tend to do what's convenient, expedient, and comfortable.

The reality is: You can't have a true meritocracy if a large percentage of your high-performing employee base is excluded from the best assignments, excluded from the mentoring and grooming that happen automatically for the well-connected or those from similar backgrounds. That's not a culture where merit determines outcomes.

CJ: **What are your thoughts on 360-degree performance reviews?**

VF: I've never met one that I liked. I have an issue with the execution, not the theory. Getting input on your performance from people with whom you interface is a good idea . . . in theory.

You have to ask, Were expectations and goals clear? Was the playing field level, meaning everyone had the proper level of support? Are you measuring something that the individual didn't know was important until the 360 degree results came back? Employees often become confused relative to what managers and colleagues expect because there are often inconsistencies in what they say the company values and what behaviors are rewarded. This lack of clarity can be a death knell for the careers of professionals of color because they're less likely to be given a second chance to demonstrate value to the business.

And it's usually the troops getting the 360-degree review, not the leaders. So, few leaders get meaningful feedback about how well they are doing the talent development and talent management portions of their jobs. Consequently, they rarely get better at setting expectations and appraising the work of team members in an unbiased fashion.

CJ: If you were to design a diversity and inclusion program, what would it look like?

VF: The process would be forward-thinking. It would not ignore the past, but it would not get hung up on what didn't happen before.

The first response to diversity gaps should no longer be "We'll implement a training program." The process would focus on vision and strategy, implementing reliable systems, holding executive-level leaders accountable for results. The focus for middle managers would be on the pragmatic issues related to making inclusion work—how to recruit a more diverse team, how to use a team's diversity to produce stronger results, how to serve a more diverse customer base.

CHAPTER FOUR

HR Is Not Your Savior

"*Paul*" *had a serious problem.* His manager was making false allegations about his engagement and effectiveness on a cross-functional project. Knowing the manager's personality and track record as he did, Paul was convinced that the allegations were the start of a smear campaign. In response, Paul quickly launched a counteroffensive, contacting Human Resources to present a fact-based counterargument supported by witnesses and documentation. As a result, HR promised to conduct an investigation.

However, rather than interviewing all the witnesses on Paul's list and poring over his documentation, HR wrapped up the "investigation" almost overnight and sided with the manager. They even suggested that *Paul* was the problem, agreeing with the manager that he wasn't up to the job and had been "overpromoted." Although HR was supposed to be investigating Paul's manager, they flipped the script and began discrediting Paul.

At another time and place, *I* filed a complaint with HR against a manager, along with a large group of my coworkers.

For too long, we'd endured an abusive boss—someone whose behavior was so horrible that even her assistant director was appalled. In fact, the assistant director was the person who initiated the complaint, but before doing so, he recruited me and a number of my colleagues, hoping there would be strength in numbers.

The complaint was filed, but HR did nothing. That is, they did nothing to address the problem. What they *did* was tell our boss about the complaint so that, shortly thereafter, she chastised us for filing it. Although her behavior improved (slightly), the situation became extremely awkward from then on. Whenever she had a chance, the manager would rub our faces in the fact that she was still there.

I've worked with some solid HR professionals: passionate human beings who really believed in their mission. They were professional, intelligent, compassionate, apolitical, and well respected by the employees. Unfortunately, I've also worked with HR people who engaged in unscrupulous behavior such as conducting one-sided investigations of complaints, fabricating excuses about why certain employees (too often, people of color) didn't receive promotions or equitable salary raises, and engaging in "tokenism" to create diverse-seeming slates of job candidates.

Regarding HR personnel, therefore, my advice is: *Do not trust until you verify.* In other words, do *not* assume that an HR person is ethical and trustworthy until you *verify* that they are. And even then, take a look at their job level to determine whether they are positioned high enough to call out bad behavior of an executive without fearing for their job.

How HR Functions

If you studied business in college or grad school, you may have taken a course on human resources. If so, you would have learned that HR works for management, not the employees. Hence, HR is not your "union rep." In fact, HR is more likely to serve management in the capacity of spin doctor, crisis manager, or "fixer" than to serve as an employee advocate. As a result, "HR can be your best friend if management is on your side. But they can be your biggest roadblock if the opposite is true," said a former coworker.

So, if you took that HR class, you were probably better prepared to manage your expectations *before* entering the workforce. You already understood what HR is and isn't. As another colleague once summarized, "During a conflict with management, I never made the mistake of thinking that HR would be helpful, and they never were."

In fairness, I'm sure many HR executives are well intentioned but often find themselves walking a tightrope. In addition to doing the right thing, they want to keep their jobs, get promoted, and enjoy professional growth. Very often, a good way to accomplish those goals is to avoid stepping on powerful toes. This explains why quite a few of my HR acquaintances never bothered to walk the tightrope. They probably decided that being fair would get them nowhere. If these people could survive by throwing someone under a bus, they would do it in a heartbeat.

Because (to quote Forrest Gump) HR is "like a box of chocolates; you never know what you're gonna get," it's imperative that professionals at every level of the organization, and especially young professionals, avoid misguided assumptions about HR and learn how to effectively engage with HR people.

In my experience, employee assumptions about HR are not always aligned with reality. One reason for this is that HR serves different functions for different people, and some of these functions contradict each other. For example, the C-suite tends to believe that HR is about risk mitigation and regulatory compliance. For them, the primary mission of the department is ensuring that the company meets its legal and regulatory obligations. Hence, in their view, HR mainly exists to protect the company.

As you move down the corporate ladder, however, you're more likely to encounter employees who believe that HR exists to shield them from abuse, whether that abuse takes the form of safety violations, sexual harassment, racism, homophobia, and other infringements of their workplace and civil rights. In theory, this assumption is correct. However, as you veterans of HR classes know, the prime directive of most HR departments is protecting the company *first*, and the employees *second*. In practice, therefore, HR usually tries to make sure that the victor in any conflict between the company and the employees is the company.

This doesn't mean that HR, when mediating a dispute between an individual manager and an employee, will always side with the manager. It *does* mean that HR will usually promote the best interests of the *company* over the best interests of any individual. If tossing a bad-seed manager into the unemployment line serves the best interests of the company, so be it. If ignoring, silencing, or firing an aggrieved employee best serves the company, it's all good. To paraphrase a mantra from *Star Trek*, HR tends to believe that "the needs of the many outweigh the needs of the few or the one." That is, unless they've been directed by someone in authority to do the opposite.

Even under ideal conditions, HR people must try to faithfully serve the company that pays their salaries while also serving employees—a balancing act that many departments fail to achieve.

Another misguided assumption is that HR does nothing but field complaints, "orient" new employees, and administer benefits. For this reason, many executives don't have a lot of respect for HR. (Another reason for the disrespect is that HR tends to be viewed as a department whose purpose is to consume, and not produce, profits.) In reality, HR's range of responsibilities includes (but is not limited to) recruiting and talent acquisition, learning and development, talent management, compensation/benefits, employee relations, and, if they're relatively progressive, diversity, equity, and inclusion. What many people don't realize, therefore, is that they could—and should—be challenging HR to meet a wider range of employee needs. After all, HR is supposed to be a service organization.

If your HR department isn't already, it should be doing the following:

- Collecting, analyzing, and reporting metrics that track employee effectiveness (as a manager, you should be able to receive answers to questions such as: "Can I see the past three years of employee engagement surveys? Have you uncovered any glaring concerns? What actions have been taken to address these concerns, and what were the results?")

* Offering leadership development training
* Educating employees on how to recalibrate their careers
* Helping workers recognize and develop "soft skills," for example, how to provide/receive feedback, how to be an emotionally intelligent leader
* Ensuring succession planning is fair and just
* Helping employees address work–life balance challenges
* Playing a central role in change-management activities
* Communicating the relevance of transferable skills
* Promoting intentional equity, diversity, and inclusion efforts by moving beyond the investigation and analysis stages (why do some HR departments continue to assess the situation when they already know that there is racism and sexism in the organization?)
* Ensuring greater transparency in how promotions are handled

One thing every employee should know is that **everything *is* negotiable and *should be* negotiated**, including the terms of your offer letter, your performance reviews, and so forth.

Case in point: I was recruited to join a company where I'd worked six years earlier, but before agreeing to return, I wanted my tenure "bridged" to ensure I was grandfathered in to the company pension plan—something new employees were not being offered. Initially, HR said it couldn't be done. However, a very senior leader was my sponsor. We'd worked together in the past, and she believed I was the perfect candidate to turn the organization around. Thanks to her sponsorship, and the fact that

I wasn't desperate to leave my current job, I was negotiating from a position of strength. So, I held out until I received my desired salary and my tenure was bridged. Now, had I been *unemployed* at the time, it would have been a different story. You'd better believe that HR would have leveraged that fact during negotiations.

In general, to effectively interact with HR, it's important to understand the role it's supposed to play in your organization. If you don't understand that role, you won't be able to utilize HR as a valuable resource. So, prior to interacting with HR, ask yourself:

1. *Why* does it exist?
2. *What* is its purpose and mission?
3. *How* does it operate?

If you don't know the answers to those questions, find out.

Once you understand the role of HR in your organization, I suggest you adopt a policy of "proactive engagement" with it by

- Requesting advice/guidance from HR before sitting down with your direct reports to discuss performance reviews or other sensitive issues. Simply ask HR for tips on how to approach those types of discussions. (There's a very good chance that your HR rep will inform your manager about your request, but that shouldn't stop you.)
- Seeking guidance and coaching from HR on various best practices.
- Soliciting input from HR on how to set performance goals tied to compensation and promotions. Ask the HR reps to provide an overview for your team or department to

ensure that everyone (managers and employees) is aligned in their view of how the process should work. Specifically ask, "What would I need to deliver to be considered for a promotion?" Establish checkpoints with your manager, and if you lack trust, keep records and loop your HR rep into the ongoing conversations and tracking.

- Inviting HR personnel to meet with you and your team on a regular basis to discuss key policies, including compensation rules, talent acquisition procedures, development opportunities within the organization, etcetera.

"Press 2 to File a Complaint"

I began my career at a time when HR was more committed to people than it is today. HR resources were visible and accessible, and you sensed that the people genuinely cared about the welfare of employees. This is not as true today. At many organizations, HR staffs have been downsized in favor of AI software, and two-way interactions between employees and HR personnel have been replaced by automated self-service models: "Press 1 for an explanation of benefits; press 2 to file a complaint, or follow this link to download the necessary forms."

Of course, this kind of automation is nothing new, and it isn't confined to HR. Not that long ago, the first person you'd see on entering a department was the receptionist. How many receptionists do you see today? For me, however, the automation of HR has been particularly striking because of (1) the *extent* of the automation, and (2) the kinds of interactions that "robots" are now called on to perform. Today, almost all employee information is contained in databases such as Human Resource Information

Systems (HRISs) and SAP Human Capital Management (SAP HCM) systems. They have become the system of record for the entire life cycle of every employee, enabling everything from individual performance management to the analysis of companywide turnover ratios.

Ideally, these systems can help (the remaining) HR people do their jobs better and faster, freeing them to devote more time to one-on-one interactions with employees. In the real world, of course, some organizations are merely replacing HR personnel with robots, stranding the employees on AI-driven hamster wheels, where they must futilely attempt to extract answers from machines.

To put it kindly, AI systems can be a burden. Some organizations expect them to do too much, and some systems have clunky user interfaces that make them very frustrating to use. These systems automatically push out deliverables to employees that enable HR to meet its obligations to the firm. In the past, HR people used to allot time in their workdays to complete these obligations. Today, *you* are the one allotting time in *your* workday to meet many of these obligations. At least supermarkets give customers a *choice* of whether to use the full-service checkout or self-service checkout. There, you at least have the option of trying to reason with a human. Good luck reasoning with a piece of software.

My perspective may reek of cynicism, but that cynicism is informed by decades of experience. And that experience tells me that most employees want and need more than what's currently offered by many HR departments. Any company saying that they didn't notice sexism or racism before the Me Too movement and George Floyd is lying. You don't need reams of data to see that there are problems when those problems are real. HR could simply draw a correlation from the number of lawsuits and settlements that have occurred in recent years. They could and should be drawing a correlation between those things and what their employee engagement surveys are telling them. If your organization has been perpetually underperforming in a particular area over a significant period, that's a bright red flag that the organization either can't do better or doesn't want to do better.

Unfortunately, I expect that an increasing number of companies will implement an HR model that's mostly automated and totally on demand, with the spin being that the new systems are "designed for you." You can take your training when you want, choose your benefits at two a.m. if you like. HR has shifted from "that department down the hall" to a largely impersonal, automated interface system and shared services center that is somehow supposed to manage important, complex, and sometimes very messy challenges. So now more than ever it's important to manage your expectations of HR because it's unlikely that anyone will be walking down the hall anytime soon to see whether you need help with your benefits selection.

The good news is that HR departments in some companies have begun developing more effective learning labs, with a focus on career development.

The bad news is that this probably isn't happening at your company.

To Manage Problems, Eliminate Emotions

I once had a colleague who would cry—or whose eyes would water—at the drop of a hat. When presented with a challenge or a predicament, she would usually describe the situation not in terms of the facts but in terms of her *feelings*: "I feel this" and "I feel that."

I understand that people react differently to stress, but "leading with your feelings" is *not* the correct way to address problems and challenges—at least, not publicly. Privately, feel free to go home—not to your office—to scream, unleash torrents of tears, break dishes, and punch holes in the drywall until it resembles a moonscape. But in discussions with bosses, colleagues, and, particularly, HR, keep your feelings out of it.

HR is there to manage factual situations and show empathy for your feelings. If you're stating your case and they keep saying, "I'm sorry you feel that way," then you're losing the argument. (At a minimum, you're not doing a good job of persuading them.)

It's hard to investigate feelings. That doesn't mean that your feelings are unimportant—just that it's difficult for someone to simultaneously manage a problem while being considerate of your feelings. More important, you don't want to acquire a reputation of being "emotional." You want HR to advocate for your growth as opposed to cautioning hiring managers about your hypersensitivity and delicate feelings.

It's okay to become emotional. As much as possible, though, keep those emotions to yourself while you're in the workplace and, instead, search for logical arguments to frame the problem and for sound strategies to resolve it. When dealing with human resources complaints, I typically framed my arguments by stating that I did X (or wanted to do X) "for the good of the business." This tactic, which I learned from my mentors, was usually quite effective.

In some situations, however, you may find that an emotional response is an asset rather than a liability. For example, if you're accused of violating one of the organization's internal policies or its code of conduct, surprise and properly placed/applied dosages of outrage may be an effective—and duly expected—response to the accusation. (Note: All major companies have codes of conduct, and if the company is publicly traded, you'll often find the code on the company website. As an example, here's Google's: https://abc.xyz/investor/other/google-code-of-conduct/.)

I recommend that you assess every situation individually, and then adopt an approach (fact-based vs. emotion-based vs. some combination of facts and emotions) that you believe will work best. Before doing this, however, first determine your goal, what you want to get out of the engagement with your boss or HR, for example, to make a strong statement, to overwhelm them with your command of the facts, to survive to play another day, or to gain empathy or respect. Just keep in mind that although HR is a department, in most instances you'll be interacting with a single individual. If you don't know this individual very well, you'll definitely want to adopt a "play it safe" strategy. And playing it safe usually means relying on the facts, not emotions.

Sometimes it's best to let silence fight your battles. Look a person in the eye while they're telling you something you don't agree with, listen closely, say thank you when they finish, and then walk away silently. I once had a situation with a manager who was a hard charger, someone I respected because he worked hard, remained polite, and was committed to the success of the team. On one occasion, however, I encountered an issue and shared my concerns about the situation, but the manager dismissed my views. Shortly thereafter, to the manager's credit, he had the humility to send an email over the course of a weekend explaining that he had a change of heart. He even closed the correspondence by apologizing for not recognizing my concern. That leader will forever have my respect—for respecting me enough to reflect on our exchange and resolve it when cooler heads prevailed.

On another occasion, a manager (one of those well-connected, overpromoted bosses) was pressuring me to demote a high-performing employee working on a high-profile program so he could replace him with a friend. I spoke to my mentor, author Cynthia Hardy, who was aware of this problematic boss and the emergency meeting he'd called to review data that did not exist. Cynthia said, "When you go into that office, leave your emotions at the door, and don't expect logic from an illogical person on an unethical mission. Pretend that you can float above your body and look down on the discussion as if it were a chessboard. Then mentally move the pieces." I did that and felt incredibly comfortable and confident. Although I didn't get everything I wanted out of that meeting, I was able to exercise far more control over the outcome than I'd expected.

What Kind of Trouble Is This?

People tackle challenges (large and small) every day, usually without thinking about them very much. If you're a pessimist, you might regard life itself as a never-ending series of challenges that must be managed before moving on to the next series of challenges.

"Soup or salad? Soup."

"Jeremy or Kathy for the role of project manager? Kathy."

Every so often, however, you'll confront a really big challenge—something so big and so fraught with emotion that the word *challenge* is too weak to describe it. You've encountered some kind of *trouble*.

How do you distinguish between a garden-variety challenge and real trouble? The examples below should help clarify the difference:

- I'm undercompensated for what I was hired to do = **Challenge**
- My colleague received a bigger raise or a larger merit increase than I did = **Challenge**
- My colleague received a bigger raise or a larger merit increase than I did because he's a man and/or he's white and/or he's the CEO's nephew = **Trouble**
- You're laying me off or I've been downsized, and I'm upset = **Challenge**
- I'm being terminated for poor performance = **Challenge**
- I'm being bypassed for high-profile opportunities because of my age = **Trouble**
- Employees are requesting a higher level of transparency around the employee calibration and ratings process = **Challenge**
- Employees are being told that the goals management approved at the beginning of the year were not impactful enough at the end of the year to merit a bonus = **Challenge**
- Members of our frontline staff in Texas have been averaging fifty hours a week but aren't being paid overtime = **Trouble**

As you undoubtedly noticed, **trouble** tends to take the form of failure to comply with the law or applicable regulations governing your industry or company, whereas **challenges** can be more ambiguous. You may have named Kathy as project manager because of her demonstrable skills and knowledge, but what if Kathy happens to be white and Jeremy believes he was bypassed for the role because he's Latino? What kind of trouble is this?

This is why it's important to adopt a proactive strategy vis-à-vis HR. It's why I recommend that you solicit advice and guidance from HR on how to set performance goals tied to compensation and promotions. It's why I suggest that you have HR provide your team or department with an overview of company policies and the code of conduct—to ensure that everyone knows how promotions, compensation, terminations, and the like should work. The best way to answer the question "What kind of trouble is this?" is to have HR answer the question for you. Better yet, avoid trouble entirely (or at least more often) by enlisting HR personnel as in-house consultants and troubleshooters when it comes to sensitive issues.

Unfortunately, depending on the type of people you're dealing with, HR may try to sweep trouble under the rug. In that case, you may need to "scream loud and raise your hand high" to someone else in authority. This is especially true when trouble takes the form of legal or regulatory violations such as sexual harassment and workplace discrimination.

However, you may also encounter situations in which discretion is the best strategy. Pick your battles wisely by first considering the environment in which you're "living" and the likely long-term impact of the words and deeds that you're contemplating. Think long and hard about the battles you can win, and which you can't win. Also, be aware that although most firms have stated policies to protect whistleblowers from retaliation, retaliation still happens.

Personally, I believe it's better to be on the right side of history, and to accept whatever retaliation comes my way, than to keep silent when an egregious injustice has been committed. It's the minor injustices that should cause you to pause and think before deciding whether to scream loud or to keep quiet and live to fight another day.

Case in point: During a private conversation that a friend ("Greg") had with a well-established and well-connected colleague, "Mr. Connected" flippantly referred to the local employees using a racially derogative term. Previously, Greg had had several challenging interactions with Mr. Connected because the latter was unfair and sometimes abusive to an employee whom they both managed. Ultimately, Greg decided to manage the situation diplomatically, knowing that his colleague had relationships at the highest levels of the organization—friends who would lie to vouch for his character. Greg realized that this was a no-win situation and that raising his hand would merely paint a target on his back. He had no faith that internal processes would resolve the problem, so he opted to keep quiet.

This isn't to say that Greg did nothing. It's possible to be silent while working behind the scenes to resolve the problem. Toward that end, Greg closely and continuously monitored how Mr. Connected engaged with employees. Among other things, Greg asked to read the performance reviews conducted by Mr.

Connected and had a trusted colleague keep an eye on him, too. The hope was that if Mr. Connected ever went too far, Greg would have the evidence in hand to win the next battle.

Strategically Leverage HR to Your Advantage

In addition to proactively engaging HR, find ways to strategically leverage it to your advantage. Again, this requires that you understand the purpose of HR within your organization, its construct, and what it is designed to deliver, as well as its goals and initiatives. For example, if the board has tasked HR with widening the leadership pipeline for diverse employees, this presents an opportunity for appropriate candidates to market themselves to HR. Learn what HR needs, identify opportunities, and marry yourself to the right opportunities.

I try to cultivate relationships with the HR people responsible for recruiting, talent acquisition, and talent management. I have coffee or cocktails with these folks to learn (at the embryonic stages) about executive-level roles that are opening up. In many organizations where I've worked, executive roles were posted only as a technicality. The recruiters would say, "For compliance reasons, we have to post this position internally for five days" or whatever the required period was. When this happened, and if the position was a good fit for me, my goal was to ensure that the internal recruiters knew me, trusted me, and were willing to advocate for me. On other occasions, they might say to the hiring managers, "Before we post this role externally, have you considered any internal candidates?" More often than not, the hiring managers were simply creating the role for someone in their personal network, but by speaking up to the HR folks, I would at least appear on their radar with an endorsement from the recruiter. Some recruiters trusted me enough to warn me off particular openings, saying, "He's not going to hire you, and to be honest, he's an asshole."

As you can see, having friends in HR can offer significant benefits. In addition to helping you identify opportunities, HR people can be your ears in the room when you aren't there. Additionally, they are often trusted advisors to the most influential people in the organization, so if you want to maintain a certain proximity to power, your friends in HR can often facilitate this.

Another way to exercise leverage with HR is to build a kick-ass professional network, internally and externally, with influence at all levels of the organization. You goal is to use that network of professional friends and allies to strategically apply pressure to internal decision-making processes. Anyone who isn't leveraging internal *and* external networks to put pressure on internal decision-making is at an extreme disadvantage.

As an example, consider one of the processes by which one tech giant recruits students for certain roles. On the one hand, they have partnerships with historically Black colleges and universities (HBCUs) to help them recruit for their engineering programs. (Students start as interns and may be offered a full-time job with the company on successful completion of a test at the end of the internship.) On the other hand, this pipeline is also open to students from other schools, including schools that would be classified as Ivies.

Consider how powerful a network can be in determining career prospects. As an example, several Big Tech firms recruit directly from the engineering programs of colleges and universities. They have formed partnerships with many historically Black colleges and universities (HBCUs) as well as many Ivy-caliber and well-funded state universities, and these schools have a direct pipeline to Silicon Valley. Students can start as interns at a tech firm and then may be offered full-time employment on successful completion of the internship, and in some cases a placement test. Opportunities are equally open to all, it seems, but HBCU grads are conspicuously missing from Silicon Valley.

At first glance, you might assume that the dearth of HBCU grads employed in the tech giants means these students simply aren't as smart or qualified as students from the other schools. But there's more to the story.

Unsurprisingly, the tech companies employ a ranking system for universities that establishes priorities for recruiting programs and budgets. The ranking criteria are not publicized, but unsurprisingly, the schools traditionally perceived as Ivy-caliber are given elite status, and others fall into lower tiers; for years, HBCUs were barely on the radar and receive little to no investment from technology firms to strengthen their STEM programs.

The upshot is, alumni of elite and high-ranking schools get hired and go on to form powerful internal networks in the tech companies that then leverage their influence over recruiting, testing, and hiring to bring in more of their graduates. This helps ensure certain universities' pipelines to Big Tech, as well as their network of "influencers," remain robust. By contrast, HBCUs are not quite as favored partners to Big Tech and therefore do not have the opportunity to establish these powerful internal networks that support and prepare and refer their graduates.

So, I repeat: If you're not leveraging networks to put pressure on the internal decision-making processes that are important to your career, you are at an *extreme* disadvantage.

Review your company's employee handbook and visit the HR department's intranet site to understand their priorities, the resources made available to employees, and preferred methods of engagement. Ask questions of your HR partners when you don't have a clear understanding, and when possible try to provide value to them by proposing a solution along with a concern or complaint.

CHAPTER FIVE

Get Smart about Money

f you've ever read a book or an article about budgeting, saving, investing, or another personal finance topic, you may have noticed that most authors simply *assume* that you actually *have* something to budget, save, and invest—that is, disposable income. Although they can take it for granted, *you* may have to work hard to ensure that you're fairly compensated. In fact, there may be times when you'll have to push hard to ensure that your compensation is tied to your actual performance, not a perceived "need" or an "ism" such as racism, sexism, or ageism. In a truly meritocratic world, equitable compensation would naturally flow to those who produce results. In *this* world, you may have to wrest it from the tight fists of the powers that be.

Obtaining Equitable Compensation

Years ago, my "Rolling Stone" manager gave me a 4 on my annual review (on the scale, 5 was the lowest rating and 1 the highest). As a result, I received just 40 percent of my bonus. His justification was that my project didn't deliver a net savings during the calendar year. This was nonsense. We were a new group in the organization, and cost savings weren't even written into any of our goals for the year. Benefits realization for the project wasn't slated to occur until the following year. Moreover, none of the programs led by my peers realized benefits during the year. Despite all this, my manager decided to apply this criterion to me and nobody else.

I escalated the matter to the CIO, who was my one-up manager, and to HR, but nothing was done. So, I escalated it further by bringing it to the attention of a very senior HR executive of color, who was appalled. He sent two communications to the CIO asking for an explanation, but he was also ignored. (Before this HR executive moved to another firm, he forwarded the communications to me so I would at least know that he'd tried and so I had something to keep in my back pocket just in case.)

If I didn't know what privilege was before, this episode taught me the real meaning. It was a blatant case of compensation that was awarded based not on performance but on something subjective (possibly racism). Unfortunately, it's not always this easy to determine whether you've been treated unfairly. Very often, the culprits don't leave fingerprints. To learn whether you're really the victim of some form of discrimination, you need evidence, which would normally consist of the communications of your bosses and peers. (Your peers might say anything from "I'm happy with what I got" or "I received my full bonus" to "It could have been better" or "I got screwed and my boss is an asshole.") Unless someone shares their communications, you're probably out of luck. And even when they *do* share, damning information is frequently couched in vague language.

Fortunately, most companies have job grades, with a compensation range tied to each grade. In theory, this information allows you to compare the compensation you received with what others who share the same grade have received. In reality, this information may not be much use. I've worked at companies where the compensation range within grades was as wide as a football field. Therefore, even if you shared the same grade with another employee, the two of you might inhabit completely different tax brackets, making it nearly impossible to prove bias.

Some progressive companies are taking steps to review compensation across the board. The goal is to ensure that employees doing the same or similar work are compensated equitably, and if not, to take corrective measures. But if you don't work for one of these organizations, this news is probably small comfort.

Still, one of the first steps you can take to ensure that your compensation is fair and performance-based is to **learn your job grade** and the associated pay range. Some companies will give you a detailed offer letter when you're hired or promoted into a new role. The letter will outline your total compensation package, including your base salary, short-term incentive (STI), and long-term incentive plan (LTIP).

Your base salary is guaranteed. However, your STI and LTIP may be tied to a target range. This is where the danger lies. The offer letter may display a total compensation package of X, but 50 percent of that compensation may take the form of variable comp tied to the target range and your performance rating for the year. In addition, the comp may also be linked to the company's overall financial performance. This is great news if the company is having a good year. In that case, your maximum payout could equal 150 percent of the target. But in years when my company wasn't doing so well, I received payments representing just 85 percent of the target, even when I received a stellar 1 rating on my performance review.

In sum, you can knock it out of the park within your department, but the variable comp you receive for that performance can be negatively affected by the poor performance of another business unit—a unit over which you have no control. In fairness, it can work both ways. Sometimes, *your* butt will be saved by another department's excellent performance.

If your manager rates you poorly, it will affect your year-end bonus, which is typically paid in Q1 of the following year. It could also impact your bonus for years to come because LTIP is usually paid out over a period of several years. I've worked at companies at which there was a three- to five-year vesting and disbursement period. Moreover, those same firms often had a three- to five-year vesting and disbursement period for some employees and an eight-year period for others. (This scheme is typical within financial services firms, with the longer vesting period usually applied to investment personnel such as wealth managers.)

The second step you should take is to sit down with your manager to discuss your goals for the year *and* the weight of those goals vis-à-vis your compensation. For example, if you have five major goals, you might agree that three of them will have the most impact, and assign a compensation value of 25 percent to each, while the remaining two goals are assigned a value of just 12.5 percent each. Personally, I believe that when goals cascade from the top, this gives you more leverage come bonus time because it enables you to draw a clear connection to the company's objectives and policies.

Finally, whenever possible, find a way to link what you do to the CEO's priorities. You can do that no matter what your level. For example, if one corporate goal is to improve the customer experience, and you manage the contact center, it's easy to make a clear connection because your work is customer-facing. In this case, you may want to set up a customer feedback survey on the telephone system so that you'll have a clear-cut way of tracking your progress on a goal that aligns with the CEO's goal. Just be sure to obtain your manager's approval in advance and weight the goal accordingly. And if you're fortunate enough to work for an organization that has skip-level meetings, be sure to share what you're doing with your boss's boss so they're aware of it and how much progress you're making.

Keep in mind, however, that even the best-laid plans don't always pay dividends. There are no guarantees. For example, I enjoyed one of the best years of my career while wrapping up a high-profile transformation project for the CEO. I was well supported by great sponsors, but when the time came for my pecuniary recognition, my boss was gone, the COO was gone, and the CEO was under attack by hostile board members. Although I had evidence of the good work I had delivered and its importance to the firm, my new manager could not have cared less. He was focused on taking care of his favorites.

Shortly thereafter, this same manager screwed over one of my colleagues. While traveling abroad, he was scheduled to meet with her for a year-end discussion, including a performance review and rating. Although he was in-country for a week, he never bothered to contact her. Instead, she had to track him down on the day he was set to return Stateside to set up a meeting. In the end, he gave her all of two minutes, during which he informed her that she was receiving a 3 rating. He gave no explanation as to why she was awarded a mediocre score, nor did he offer any recommendations on what she should do to receive a higher rating in the coming year. This woman dedicated a year of her life to working overseas only to receive a "meh" rating from an executive who didn't give a shit about his employees.

My friends, it's managers like this who have made it necessary for managers like me to write chapters about how to obtain equitable compensation.

Wage and Hiring Disparities Reveal a Broken System

According to 2014 statistics from the U.S. Department of Labor, 76 percent of human resource managers are women. Even more impressive, given the gender gap at executive levels, women comprise 49 percent of HR officers among the top one hundred corporate employers in the United States. All told, 71 percent of HR professionals are female, according to Namely's HR Careers Report.[1] Almost two-thirds (65 percent) of HR professionals identified as white. The next highest representations were Asian at 12 percent and Hispanic at 10 percent.[2]

In sum, whites, women, and Asians are overrepresented in the profession. Hispanics are severely underrepresented, and African Americans barely register as a percentage because their numbers are so low.

Ironically, although many white female executives have been turning up the volume on calls for gender equality, as a group, they've been less outspoken when it comes to racial equity in the workforce. Systemic racism has been a major success impediment for African Americans and Latinos. Corporations have failed to equitably hire, promote, and compensate African Americans, Latinos, and other people of color. The numbers tell us that white women have been in positions to effectuate change, or call it out, but it took a video of a man being murdered over the course of 8:46 minutes to spur them to action.

A coaching client of mine once shared his frustration with the system by stating, "I've been disappointed time and time again. There are far too many white women in HR and corporate America overall who share the mindset of the same white men that they complain about, while having the luxury of playing a damsel in distress."

Another colleague complained, "This legacy of nepotism has continued under their watch and it's very disappointing. They know that the racism exists; the data is there along with the Glassdoor reviews."

This is not an attack on anyone—merely an observation. We can't fix what's broken until we acknowledge that it's broken.

Even during periods of unprecedented economic growth, and despite Black academic achievement, the pay gap between Blacks and whites remains wide. (See Table 5.1.) The Black–white wage gap grew from roughly 22 percent in 2000 to 24 percent in 2007 to 27 percent in 2019.[3] (And that last spike occurred after ten years of economic recovery.) As the field of data science grows, companies should immediately deploy and embed data scientists into their HR functions to help address these equity issues.

As a husband to a beautiful wife, a loving son to an octogenarian mom who poured her everything into me, big brother to a sister who shares my birth date, father to four daughters who have excelled in academics at some of the nation's top universities, grandfather to a precious granddaughter, and godfather to three dynamic god-daughters who all work in corporate America, my biggest concern for them is racial, not gender, discrimination. But both are extremely important, and the history and data justify my concern.

Table 5.1 Black–White Wage Gaps
Widen across Multiple Measures

	2000	2007	2019
Average	21.8%	23.5%	26.5%
LOW-, MIDDLE-, AND HIGH-WAGE WORKERS			
10th percentile	6.2%	8.7%	9.0%
Median	20.8%	22.3%	24.4%
95th percentile	28.0%	28.3%	34.7%
WORKER EDUCATION LEVEL			
High school	15.3%	17.4%	18.3%
College	17.2%	19.2%	22.5%
Advanced degree	12.5%	16.7%	17.6%
Regression-based*	10.2%	12.2%	14.9%

* Regression-adjusted wage gap, controlling for age, gender, education, and region.

Source: Elise Gould, "Black–White Wage Gaps Are Worse Today Than in 2000," Economic Policy Institute, February 27, 2020, https://www.epi.org/blog/black-white-wage-gaps-are-worse-today-than-in-2000/.

Escaping the Nuthouse

You've probably heard the expression, "Some people work to live, while others live to work." Well, I'd like to append this adage with the following: "and thanks to poor financial planning, others become indentured servants to the company."

I've met countless people who, for a variety of reasons, are practically chained to their desks. Don't become one of them.

Start planning now for how you'd survive if things became so bad at your organization that you needed to escape the nuthouse. Of course, if you *want* to be an indentured servant, there are plenty of routes to choose. You can: live beyond your means; experience a sudden loss of household income if you or your partner lose a job; send your kids to pricey private schools; wake up one morning to discover that your parents require expensive eldercare; buy too much house just before the market "corrects" and pushes you under water; or make a bad investment that leaves you desperate for liquidity. Whatever the cause, the result is the same: it's much harder to quit a job when you're always one paycheck away from insolvency.

To avoid this fate, develop a personal finance game plan the moment you enter the workforce. The younger, the better. There are tons of books on how to manage your personal finances, so I won't go into detail. I'll simply note that if you should ever need a passport to leave the potential asylum where you've landed, it's imperative to build an emergency fund.

My advice? Max out your 401(k) as soon as you join corporate America to take advantage of any company matching, and watch your money grow. Keep your credit card debt low—if only to minimize the impact on your FICO score—and don't live beyond your means. If possible, live *below* your means to ensure more flexibility. Cash savings and low debt are key to your future freedom.

If the Covid-19 pandemic has taught us anything, it's that the world can change in an instant. Don't take anything for granted. You may think it's easy for me to dole out such advice, but I've learned many of these lessons the hard way. I made a *lot* of financial missteps in the past. So, when I say that getting an affordable life insurance policy is a whole lot easier and cheaper at age twenty-five than thirty-five, I know what I'm talking about. The sooner you begin saving, the sooner you'll be able to make life decisions that lead to happiness, dignity, and a life based on integrity.

One of my old mentees ("Alex"), a dynamic, big-hearted man with a strong inclination toward service leadership, is a tech executive. If God were to design the perfect prototype for the roles Alex has had, it would be him. Unfortunately, he has twice found himself in very toxic work environments, organizations where white privilege and passive-aggressive behavior ran rampant. One morning, before one of our biweekly coaching sessions, he sent a text informing me that he'd had enough. He was going to quit his job. He'd sat down with his family and his financial advisor, and they supported his decision to create more value in his life—a desire that superseded his desire for financial security. He needed to leave immediately, and he did.

I was disappointed to hear of the torment that he was experiencing but also incredibly proud of him for taking control of the situation before irreparable harm was done. I've worked with a number of African Americans who have experienced corporate PTSD. I've dealt with this issue myself, having developed an ulcer early in my career, and I'm infuriated that so many large institutions allow their employees to be abused. In most cases, either the senior management knows that abusive behavior is occurring or they should know. The higher-ups have vast networks, methods, and mechanisms for determining what's really happening on their watch. There's absolutely no excuse for claiming ignorance. So, I was proud that Alex had taken my advice and had prepared an escape plan.

Louis Pasteur once said, "Fortune favors the prepared mind." An excellent point. I would merely add—per the old Roman saying—that fortune *also* favors the bold (*Audentis Fortuna iuvat*). Although preparation is essential, you must also summon the courage to actually follow through with your plans when the time comes. Not everyone can muster this kind of bravery. Many employees would rather work with the devil they know than face the unknown.

Case Study: Tom Bridgeforth: Escaping the Matrix

I came across this article on LinkedIn written by a former colleague, whom I respect abundantly. He was dealing with the same crap a number of us have had to deal with, and he spoke his truth after liberating himself by taking the entrepreneurship route.

After more than 20 years in corporate America, I realized that I could not do this anymore. The endless organization restructuring, the changes in direction and jockeying for position as leaders came and went, the layoffs, the millions of dollars wasted on projects that would never succeed, etc. I was in the movie *The Matrix*, living in a world that did not feel real, knowing there had to be something more out there.

Throughout my career, I considered pursuing an entrepreneurial path, but there was always a good reason (excuse) not to take the risk. I didn't have enough capital. I didn't have time. I had young kids. I had grown up believing it was safer to be in a big established company than out on your own, with advantages such as good pay, benefits, and stability.

Well, last year, my employer was kind enough to eliminate my position. I mean that sincerely. Getting the severance payout was good, but more valuable was the free time to contemplate what I wanted to do next. I decided that while looking for a new job, I would also explore some entrepreneurial options. Very quickly I realized how unhappy I was trying to network into a job, sending résumés to recruiters, and reviewing job postings. On the other hand, I felt exhilarated researching business ventures. But then the negative self-talk creeped in, with all the excuses of why this was not the right time. Then I remembered something I read in a Stephen Covey book. It was about imagining your 80th birthday party. If you got up to speak, what accomplishments would you talk about, what regrets would you have, etc. I played out three different scenarios.

In the first, I imagined that I started my own business and had been widely successful. I thought how good I would feel speaking to my family, business partners, employees, and maybe even some customers in attendance. For the second scenario, I imagined the business had crashed horribly, draining my savings and leaving me unprepared for retirement. However, I would share great stories of the adventures that led to my downfall, right before I rushed off to resume my shift as a greeter at Wal-Mart.

In the third scenario, I imagined that I had stayed in the corporate world. At that birthday party, I would reflect on the interesting jobs I had held, but I would also lament the constant concern about the next layoff, how much time I missed with my family because of all the travel, and how empty I had felt just being a cog in a giant machine. I imagined the sense of regret and all the feelings of "what if" that would haunt me.

It was clear to me that it was better to take the risk, either succeeding or failing, than to not try at all. But to be honest, I had known this deep down inside for years. And that brings me back to *The Matrix*. A line in the movie says "There is a difference between knowing the path and walking the path." As I firmly put my feet on the entrepreneurial path, all the barriers I had seen in the past quickly fell. In mere weeks, I had a list of business ventures to pursue, developed a network of entrepreneurs who could guide me, and figured out how to raise my capital. Before I could blink, I was moving into my new office and opening up for business.

I share my story not out of a sense of pride. I am actually embarrassed at how many years I wasted knowing (and talking) about the path, but not walking it. I share my story to inspire others to unplug from the "corporate matrix" and start pursuing their own entrepreneurial dreams.[4]

When it comes to managing money, there are an infinite number of mistakes you *could* make. Below, however, are the mistakes that most people *do* make, so be on guard for them:

- **Failing to obtain professional advice.** If you don't *really* know what you're doing with regard to money management and investments, don't try to save a few dollars by going it alone. In the long run, it pays to consult professional money managers, financial advisors, accountants, and tax specialists. (Provided, of course, that you pick competent ones.)

- **Becoming overleveraged.** Believe it or not, many people who receive generous paychecks are living hand to mouth. Some of them just don't know it yet. That's because it's oh-so-easy to continually "upgrade" your lifestyle with every salary raise until one day—often, when thoughts of retirement first occur—you discover you have no investable assets. By that point, it may be too late to create a portfolio that can support you in the manner to which you're accustomed, post-retirement.

- **Poor (or no) budgeting.** The rule of thumb is that 50 percent of your income should be allocated to pay fixed costs, while 30 percent can be spent on discretionary items, and *20 percent should be saved.*

- **Overinvesting in company stock.** Because shares in company stock are easy to obtain, often at a discounted rate, many employees concentrate too large a percentage of their savings in this investment vehicle. The bad news is that it can be tricky to liquidate this asset because they are usually restricted shares. Even if the company is doing fabulously and you're able to quickly sell your shares, capital gains taxes will wipe out a tidy proportion of the investment.

- **Failing to separate personal wealth from business wealth.** This is especially true for "mom & pop"-sized entrepreneurs. Too many business owners comingle their personal and business assets, which can cause them to believe that they have more liquid assets available than they really do.

How do you prevent these mistakes, or, if you've already made some of them, how can they be corrected? The answer is to establish a financial plan for all aspects of your life, and then *follow the plan*. That way, your purchases will be planned and properly budgeted, protecting you from overspending. If you start to deviate from the plan, resist the temptation. It's as simple as that.

Your long-term financial goals are up to you. My only recommendation is that you establish goals that will transport you to wherever your "happy place" happens to be, whether that's peace of mind through financial freedom, early retirement, generational wealth building, college funds for the grandkids, or simply living mortgage free. Decide what's important to you, and create a plan to accumulate and grow your assets so that you and your family can enjoy the life you want.

Having a sound investment plan gives you financial flexibility and puts you in the position of working because you *want* to, not because you *have* to. It affords you the opportunity to be more selective in the roles, companies, and people you choose to work with and, if a situation no longer suits you, to leave with an abundance of dignity.

- Be disciplined and avoid unnecessary lifestyle inflation.
- Create a budget.
- Be conscious of your goals.
- Be conscious of where your dollars are going.
- Do all this, and the puzzle pieces will fall into place.

Do stick to the plan, but keep in mind that this doesn't mean that you can't (or shouldn't) make refinements along the way. You may have to periodically adjust the plan to accommodate changing realities.

Don't invest too much in any one stock, and don't spend cash on anything and everything you want. Also, be aware that some debt is good debt. For example, if your current mortgage is costing you only 4 percent a year, it makes no sense to pay it down (or off) with money from your investment portfolio, especially if that money is earning a return of 14 percent to 16 percent annually. That's bad money management, and (in some circumstances) so is using cash for a major purchase (e.g., a car) when interest rates are low or very reasonable.

I used equity from my first home to purchase investment properties; then used the equity in the investment properties to purchase a retirement home and family compound—long before retirement. The investment is important for my wife and me. We wanted to have a space for our parents, children, grandchildren, and siblings to create treasured moments. One of my mentors, corporate executive and philanthropist Reginald Van Lee, built a place in Texas for his family to come together. He was inspired after a visit to the Kennedy Compound, which also inspired me. Another goal for me was to establish a business where I'd enjoy working after my corporate career was over, and another goal was making sure that my children graduated from college unburdened by student loan debt. Perhaps these goals will inspire you, just as some of my mentors' goals inspired me.

I would never be so bold (or foolish) as to recommend *specific* investments, but there are certain financial instruments that everyone should consider—these are investments with successful track records. Therefore, I *do* suggest that you include at least some of the following in your portfolio:

- Mutual funds
- Bonds
- Real estate
- Art (provided you know what you're doing and you also enjoy art for art's sake). My art will always be worth what I paid because I love every piece. Because it has intrinsic value to me, I see it as a good investment, regardless of what the market might say.
- Individual stocks (provided you're a knowledgeable investor)

Avoid any investment vehicle you don't *fully* understand, such as cryptocurrencies or private equity. Also, be careful about investing in certain actively managed mutual funds. You'll pay a fee for the "active management," and with few exceptions, such funds frequently underperform index funds and other passively managed funds. Unless you know what you're doing, the fees can gobble up your returns. Finally, you may want to avoid annuities. I have a colleague in his early sixties who thought it was a good idea to put all his money into an annuity. What he didn't realize was that he was giving up his rights to the assets. There are other ways to accomplish the same financial goals without giving up control over principal. For folks who want peace of mind, annuities may be a good deal, but I would steer clear of them.

While you're mapping out your future, don't overlook indirect and nonfinancial investments. Some of these can have an equally profound (or more profound) impact on your future. I'm talking about investing your time, energy, and money in such things as personal and professional friendships, your physical and mental health (including leisure-time activities), mentoring (an investment of time in people), and social causes or charities that are important to you. Many people overlook these investments because the benefits seem intangible, but believe me, they can make a huge difference when it comes to your future success. I have no idea where I'd be today had it not been for some of the friendships I've forged over the years. More than once, my friends and allies supported me during difficult times and alerted me to major opportunities that I would otherwise have never known about.

Avoid Shopaholism (Unless You Can Afford It)

Like most conditions to which the suffix *-holism* or *-holic* has been affixed, society generally holds a negative view of shopaholism and shopaholics. Very often, the shopaholic is either pitied—as someone who is "obviously" trying to fill a deep emotional or spiritual void through overconsumption—or classified as a moral degenerate who refuses to control their spending. I have a more nuanced view of shopaholics. In my opinion, there's nothing wrong with being a shopaholic if you can truly afford it. There are folks out there with more money than they could spend in a lifetime or two, and it's not my job to preach the virtues of thrift. If someone works hard, they should be able to enjoy the fruits of their labor. If you have (say) $69 million that you don't know what to do with, and you'd like to spend it on a digital artwork or a virtual real estate empire, have at it! For most of us, however, shopaholism is an unaffordable indulgence.

Many young professionals are keen to buy things that will boost their status, such as expensive cars, homes, clothing, jewelry, vacations, and that help them "keep up with the Joneses." Other people simply have expensive tastes. I have a dear friend, of a certain age, who has $120,000 in an investment account. She shared with me that she wanted to take $7,500 out of service (money that's earning more money) to buy a designer bag and shoes that she could wear to a celebrity gala. You don't have to be Suze Orman to know that's not a wise decision.

Another friend, a corporate attorney, was earning a nice salary. He had plenty of money. But he also loved luxury travel and luxury cars, so he bought them. The result? Today, he can no longer afford the retirement lifestyle that he wants. Instead of planning for the future, he decided to live for the moment, a moment that (in hindsight) wasn't worth the cost of admission.

Even if you're not spending a fortune on discretionary purchases, and even if your tastes aren't causing you to live paycheck to paycheck, unchecked spending can easily lead to disaster. It takes just one unforeseen event, such as a sudden job loss, to wipe out your retirement savings.

If you're concerned that you may be a shopaholic, consult the list of warning signs below:

- Are you living paycheck to paycheck, even though you're well compensated?
- Have you maxed out your credit cards?
- Are you obtaining new cards to help pay off your existing cards?
- Do you carry balances on your cards?
- Are you always on the lookout for lower-interest cards?
- Are you applying for loans to buy things that you shouldn't have to borrow for?

If you said *yes* to any of these questions, you may have a problem, and *now* is the time to do something about it.

An Interview with Wealth Manager Mark Smith

Financial advisor Mark Smith is recognized by Forbes as one of the top next-generation advisors in the country.

CJ: Do you have an example of someone who became an indentured servant because of their finances?

MS: I know a number of corporate executives and attorneys who have climbed the ranks of their professions and now earn a comfortable mid-six-figure to seven-figure salary. In the process, they adjusted their lifestyle to that salary level. Now they can no longer save because the money going in is the same amount going out. The rent in Manhattan went from $3,000 or $4,000 a month to $12,000 or $13,000 per month because you have a penthouse, a doorman, a parking space, etcetera. The goal is to live below your means so that you always have discretionary income to invest, pay down debt quicker, and build wealth. This positions you well to quit your job because you now have the financial flexibility and freedom to quit your job and launch a business or invest in a number of businesses that will yield meaningful dividends.

CJ: What are your top recommendations for enabling people to escape the nuthouse?

MS: You should not have more than 25 percent of your salary going out for rent. Depending on where you live (New York, San Francisco, Los Angeles, etc.) and your salary level, that might not be possible. If so, then you should consider a roommate, or not living in the city center.

If you're spending more than [25 percent], it will become increasing difficult to save money and transition from being a renter to a buyer.

If you're looking to put away money to invest in a business or launch your own business, you not only have to put away money for retirement, but you have to put away money in savings. Maxing out your 401(k) plan is great, but you can't access it without a penalty unless you're 59½ years old. Most of my clients who have been in corporate America for over ten years have most of their wealth tied up in illiquid vehicles like 401(k) plans. Which is great, as long as you live to sixty. But what do you do between the ages of thirty and sixty? You have to live, buy cars, home, tuition, vacations, start a business, etcetera, and none of that money can come out of your 401(k) plan. You can borrow up to $50,000 from your 401(k) plan, but I wouldn't do that unless I was buying a home, because that's an asset that's likely to appreciate, but definitely not for something like a car or a vacation.

Make sure you are around people who are like-minded from a financial discipline perspective, so you are not tempted to keep up with the Joneses, looking like a millionaire while being broke.

CJ: For many young people, financial planning is something they'll eventually get to. What can we do to make them more serious about their finances?
MS: Sometimes what turns the lightbulb on are life-changing events like the birth of a child. Then, all of a sudden, they say: "Wow, how much is child care, or private school, or an apartment with an extra bedroom for a nursery?"

If we've learned anything from the pandemic, it is the importance of funding an emergency account to the equivalent of eight months' salary. If you're married and your spouse is in a different industry, six months' salary should suffice. You can't responsibly initiate a conversation about investing until that emergency account is funded, and even then, a wealth manager will require $250,000 for starters. Folks I know in New York City between the ages of thirty and forty typically have about $100,000 in liquid assets—municipal bonds, CDs, stocks, and cash.

Prioritize your finances in the following order:

- Emergency fund
- 401(k) plan
- Investments

This process puts you on the path of financial freedom, or as my friends say: "Fuck You" money, which means you can tell your abusive manager to "go kick rocks," and start your own business because you have money in the bank.

And when you're dating, you can't allow the majority of your discretionary income to go to entertainment—orchestra seats, dinner twice a week at the likes of Nobu's or Mr. Chow's, exotic vacations, gifts like Gucci and Chanel purses. The . . . material things yield less than fifty cents on the dollar in the secondary market.

CJ: Name a big money management mistake that a lot of people make.

MS: First, know your benefits package inside out. A common mistake is that most folks don't understand their benefits plan, and they don't take advantage of significant tax-saving opportunities—for example, with an HSA [health savings account] Flex Spending Account, the Roth component of their 401(k) plan, etcetera. Why is this important? Because it goes in tax free and comes out tax free, and that can be a huge saving opportunity. It's a great way to legally avoid paying unnecessary taxes, which most folks don't capitalize on, but these are the only way you can affect your taxes as a W2 employee.

The second biggest mistake is biting off more than you can chew with regard to a mortgage, taxes, insurance, utilities, upkeep, etcetera. This is a result of laziness or negligence.

A good financial advisor will ask to see your benefits package. If you don't have that material, go through the information thoroughly on the company website.

CJ: What should a reader's long-term planning goal be?
MS: That varies from person to person. Some folks never plan on retiring, and others have the day marked on their calendar. If it's the latter, you'll need a very specific plan. You can go on one of the more than several sites that will help you create a financial plan based on a dollar value that you define for retirement. Make sure you consistently update your financial plan because it's a living, breathing document. You should recalibrate and refine your plan as things change.

CJ: Do you have any anecdotes about shopaholics?

MS: Unfortunately, I have a number of those stories. I know a person who won the lottery and began spending a million dollars a year and is now broke. I know a professional athlete who had a $40 million guaranteed contract, and that person will be broke by year's end.

CJ: What are the warning signs of shopaholism?

MS: Making regular purchases of more than $1,000 on things you don't need. The average person can't afford to spend $300 twice a week on dinner. Personally, I don't buy expensive items unless they are tied to a professional achievement, like a promotion. That way, it feels special.

CJ: Are there ways to cure shopaholism?

MS: Using a debit card is a potential cure, as opposed to kicking the can down the road on your $50,000 line of credit on your cards. You can also:

- Leave the credit cards out of your wallet.
- Use cash. If you can't pay your rent because you bought something you couldn't afford, that wakes you up, big time.
- Use PayPal or Venmo, but don't link a credit card to Venmo.

CJ: What are your top investment recommendations?

MS: Before you have enough money to get a financial advisor, the cheapest thing to do is buy exchange-rated funds—index funds that track the S&P 500, the Euro Stoxx 50, and the MSCI Emerging Markets Index. I would recommend a percentage split broken out as follows:

- 50 percent U.S.
- 25 percent Euro
- 25 percent emerging markets

If you have those three index funds, you should be good until you have over $250,000 to hire a financial advisor. These index funds are low cost. Every month, you can put a set amount into those funds, set it and forget it. You don't have to worry about what the market is doing. This way, you can continue to focus on your job and saving.

CJ: What kind of investments should you avoid?

MS: Restaurants (or any business, if you don't know what you're doing) unless you're partnering with Marcus Samuelson, Bobby Flay, or Wolfgang Puck. I'm totally not against crypto, but I caution you to do your research and monitor the market. If you choose to go down the path, your crypto allocation should never be higher than what you have in gold. For example, if you have 5 percent in gold, your crypto should be 5 percent or lower.

Keep in mind, too, that real estate is only an asset when it's generating money. If you're just paying upkeep, it's a liability—until/unless you sell it for a profit.

> If you think you're going to be in a neighborhood for twenty years, and your kids will go to school there, it makes sense to buy. If you're single or married with no kids, and not committed to an area for the long term, consider renting.

Managing your money and managing your career go hand in hand. If you're diligent, you will find that your path to freedom is a lot brighter because it's well lit with options of opportunity. Whether it's taking a sabbatical to travel the world, going back to school for a PhD, or opening an artisan craft shop. The key is for money not to be the impediment.

CHAPTER SIX

Juggling Work and Life Is Harder Than You Think

W*hen I was born in the 1960s,* economists promised us a future in which ever-increasing productivity would enable us to work fewer hours and enjoy more leisure time. This seemed like a perfectly reasonable thing to promise. All the trend lines were pointing in that direction.

At the time, the term *work–life balance* didn't exist. There was no need for such a term. Whereas our great-grandparents and great-great-grandparents had worked an average of seventy hours a week, those hours started falling in the early twentieth century, and they kept falling. By 1950, the average workweek for a manufacturing-sector employee had dropped to 40.5 hours. In the early 1950s, one economist even predicted that industrial workers would soon enjoy workweeks of thirty hours or less.[5]

But a funny thing happened on the way to our leisure-packed future. "After declining for most of the [twentieth] century, the share of employed American men regularly working more than 50 hours per week began to increase around 1970. This trend has been especially pronounced among highly educated, high-wage, salaried, and older men. . . . Whereas a century ago, the lowest-paid workers worked the longest hours, today the longest hours are worked by the top 10 percentile of earners."[6]

Since the 1970s, work has been trying to take over our lives again, especially the lives of high achievers: "Elite managers were once 'organization men,' cocooned by lifelong employment in a corporate hierarchy that rewarded seniority above performance. Today, the higher a person climbs on the org chart, the harder she is expected to work. Amazon's 'leadership principles' call for managers to have 'relentlessly high standards' and to 'deliver results.' The company tells managers that when they 'hit the wall' at work, the only solution is to 'climb the wall.'"[7]

Greater Expectations

What the hell happened? Did America's professionals suddenly decide they'd had enough leisure and greatly preferred spending more time in the office and less time with friends and family? Hardly. In fact, my research and personal experience indicate that the opposite is true. As author and Yale Law School professor Daniel Markovits recently observed:

> Americans who work more than 60 hours a week report that they would, on average, prefer 25 fewer weekly hours. They say this because work subjects them to a "time famine" that, a 2006 study found, interferes with their capacity to have strong relationships with their

spouse and children, to maintain their home, and even to have a satisfying sex life. A respondent to a recent Harvard Business School survey of executives proudly insisted, "The 10 minutes that I give my kids at night is one million times greater than spending that 10 minutes at work." Ten minutes!

[But] the capacity to bear these hours gracefully, or at least grimly, has become a criterion for meritocratic success.[8]

What the hell happened is basically this: beginning in the 1970s and through the 1980s, a new corporate culture emerged in the United States—a "meritocratic" culture in which high-earning professionals were expected to demonstrate their "dedication" to the organization by logging longer and longer hours at the office and on the road.

By the time I entered the corporate world, this "meritocratic" culture had evolved to the point where many executives were competing to see who could achieve the greatest work–life *imbalance* in the hope of "winning" the race to the top. Today, many executives sacrifice their personal lives by working ridiculously long hours. Why? Because *it's required of them*. Starting in business school and law school, if not earlier, people are conditioned to expect that their lives will be consumed by work and that this state of affairs is the natural order of things.

Of course, expectations vary from industry to industry, and from one company culture to the next, but in general, the legal and financial services professions have been hardest hit.

As Professor Markovits noted:

In 1962 . . . the American Bar Association could confidently declare, "There are . . . approximately 1,300 fee-earning hours per year" available to the normal lawyer. In 2000, by contrast, a major law firm pronounced with equal confidence that a quota of 2,400 billable hours, "if properly managed," was "not unreasonable," which is a euphemism for "necessary for having a hope of making partner." Because not all the hours a lawyer works are billable, billing 2,400 hours could easily require working from 8 a.m. until 8 p.m. six days a week, every week of the year, without vacation or sick days. In finance, "bankers' hours"—originally named for the 10-to-3 business day fixed by banks from the 19th century through the mid-20th century . . . have given way to the ironically named "banker 9-to-5," which begins at 9 a.m. on one day and runs through 5 a.m. on the next.[9]

In the long run, this level of work–life imbalance is probably unsustainable. Although it remains to be seen whether the next generation of bankers, lawyers, and others will call a halt to the madness, as noted by Kate Kelly and Lananh Nguyen in the *New York Times* in 2021, there are signs that they have already had enough:

> For decades, investment banking . . . was one of Wall Street's most prestigious careers, glorified in 1980s best sellers by writers like Tom Wolfe and Michael Lewis. Thousands of young hopefuls applied every year for a chance to start careers at Goldman Sachs, JPMorgan, Salomon Brothers and other banks as analysts. . . .

They embraced the long hours and grunt work in exchange for the prestige of jobs that eventually paid millions. In turn, each analyst class provided banks with a reliable pipeline of talent.

But new college graduates are increasingly unwilling to put themselves through the strenuous two-year analyst program, despite starting pay that can reach $160,000. . . . "It's kind of like going through boot camp," said Ben Chon, a 27-year-old entrepreneur whose YouTube video about leaving his job as a health care banker in JPMorgan Chase's San Francisco office, posted in February, has garnered more than 100,000 views.

Mr. Chon said he appreciated all that he had learned as an analyst, but added: "You don't have control of your lifestyle, and you're working even when you don't want to."

In a recent Instagram survey . . . 79 percent of the 139 respondents said they thought banking would be a less desired career in the future than when they had joined it. And in February, 13 analysts at Goldman showed their superiors a PowerPoint presentation describing brutally long hours and their declining health.

"The sleep deprivation, the treatment by senior bankers, the mental and physical stress . . . I've been through foster care and this is arguably worse," one of the unnamed analysts surveyed in the presentation said.[10]

Guard the Pillars of Your Life

As a current or aspiring member of the professional or managerial class, you've probably logged your fair share of all-nighters already (in school and in the office). Therefore, you may *think* you're prepared to juggle your personal and professional lives. Maybe you've even conducted mental "simulations" to determine how you'd maintain a healthy work–life balance going forward, projecting yourself into various future scenarios in which you're challenged by increasing workloads, responsibilities, and other demands on your time.

It's good to practice. It's good to mentally prepare for what the future may hold. But no matter how vivid your imagination or how sharp your planning skills, you can never fully prepare for the mental and physical toll that the stress and long hours will have on you—month after month, year after year, decade after decade.

If you've ever run a marathon, you know that, as important as it is to plan the race and visualize yourself overcoming obstacles, no amount of planning or visualization can prepare you for the first time you "hit the wall"—the moment in the race when you've depleted your glycogen reserves (chemical energy) and are suddenly overwhelmed by feelings of fatigue and negativity. Make no mistake. Preparation *is* invaluable, and so is having a strong support system on hand (in the form of family and friends) to cheer you on and raise your flagging spirits. But, ultimately, you have to first *experience* the wall to learn how to successfully overcome it in the future.

The same is true of your career. You may *think* you know what you're getting into, and you may *think* you've anticipated every challenge, but you can't possibly prepare for every curveball that life will hurl your way. And you won't really know how best to manage the big challenges until you actually *experience* some of them. And when those big challenges arrive, you're going to need a strong support system—friends, colleagues, mentors, and the like—to help guide you and raise your sagging spirits. This is one of the key reasons why it's so important to maintain a healthy work–life balance. If you become so unbalanced that you allow your personal relationships to atrophy or die, you may have no support system to lean on when the time comes—and that time *will* come.

Think of your life (both personal and professional) as a house supported by foundational pillars. You may have more (or fewer) pillars than I've identified below, but in my life, these pillars include:

1. My family and extended family (spouse, children, grand-parents, cousins, uncles and aunts, etc.)
2. My spiritual beliefs and values (especially service to others)
3. My education (formal and informal)
4. My physical and mental health

If one pillar begins to crumble, the house becomes unstable and is in danger of collapsing. Or, if you prefer another analogy, think of your life as a car. If all the tires are in good condition and properly inflated, the ride will be smooth and safe, and the car will take you to your desired destination. If the tire pressure is uneven, this will lead to poor performance and, potentially, a catastrophic accident.

Take it from someone who's been a member of the workforce for more than forty years: *It is crucial to maintain a healthy work–life balance.* If you don't spare enough time for sleep, exercise, personal relationships, and a robust spiritual life (whatever form that takes), working long hours for six to seven days a week *will* erode your physical and mental well-being. Someone who routinely misses family events, spends few or no waking hours with a significant other, skips church or synagogue or meditation, and rarely finds time to eat right and exercise is someone who is slowly sawing off the pillars of their house.

I'm not suggesting that you turn down promotions to spend more time with your spouse or thumb your nose at the boss by regularly walking out the door at five o'clock sharp to attend every one of your children's school plays. I *am* recommending that you find some time to actually live a life worth living—one that takes place outside the four walls of your office or virtual work environment.

I host a monthly restorative circle support group with eight Black executives. During one discussion, we talked about how important it had become, as we grew older and watched our parents age and pass on and our children move into adulthood, to savor the time we spend with family. More than once, I've hopped on a redeye back from the West Coast to go on a class trip with my girls or watch them portray a tree in a school play. Why? Because it was important to *them*. When I graduated high school, neither my mom nor dad, who were recently divorced, could attend. My grandma, brother, and a close friend were there to support me, and that meant the world. (To this day, it bothers me that I have no pictures with them from that day.)

Ikigai (Westernized Version)

A healthy work–life balance allows you to achieve your work and career goals without sacrificing the other things that you deem important in your life, that is, the pillars of family and friends, self-care, an intellectual and spiritual life, cultural events, and other mainstays.

To keep my balance, I subscribe to *ikigai*, a Japanese concept that means "a reason for being." The word refers to having a direction or purpose in life, something that makes one's life worthwhile and toward which an individual takes spontaneous and willing actions that provide them with satisfaction and a sense of meaning.

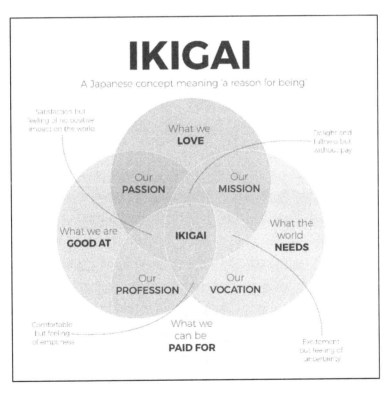

Source: "How Ikigai Can Be Applied to Early Stage Companies," WeAreHowDoI.com, April 5, 2018, https://wearehowdoi.com/news/2018/6/1/how-ikigai-can-be-applied-to-early-stage-companies.

Waking up each and every day to perform important but mundane tasks can zap your zest for life if you don't have balance. By contrast, establishing goals that encompass each pillar of life, and striking an appropriate balance among those pillars, allows you to seamlessly transition from one area of interest or importance to the next. You'll set yourself up to consistently achieve incremental progress in every area, from career advancement and keeping up with friends and family to serving the community or gaining proficiency in a musical instrument that you always wanted to learn.

You'll experience ebbs and flows and ups and downs in the course of your career. And it's during the rough patches that you will really appreciate, and benefit from, training your focus on the other pillars of your life. After a tough day at work, few things are more enjoyable than going out for drinks with a close friend to vent about the boss and your coworkers, celebrate a win at the office, or returning home to that "special someone" to enjoy a quiet dinner. Even something as simple as taking your dog for an evening walk in the park or watching your cat try to catch the beam of light from a laser pointer can help you regain badly needed perspective. It's important, now and again, to spend a few minutes living in the moment. These moments can help you find joy in the so-called little things that life has to offer. I say "so-called" because as you grow older, many of those little moments will become some of your most precious memories, while the "big stuff"—stuff you spent so much time worrying about and stressing over—has been completely forgotten.

Without proper work–life balance, however, the pillars will crack and eventually topple, leaving you with few—or no—people, causes, hobbies, interests, or passions on which to focus your attention during the bad times, or the good times. Few things are more depressing than returning home to an empty apartment after a rocky day, with no friends to call or visit, no significant other to help you "decompress," no cat, dog, hamster, or parakeet to play with, and no avocation, sporting event, or cultural happening to distract you from your work troubles. Without work–life balance, your world will steadily shrink until, before you know it, you actually dread the arrival of the holidays because you have nobody to see and nothing (but work) to look forward to.

Having the proper balance across your life pillars (or value system) forces you to periodically shift focus as you switch from one activity to the next. It allows you to enjoy and appreciate positive change, which is great for maintaining a positive attitude and outlook, for stimulating new ideas, and for creating cross-pollination opportunities.

Your Experience May Vary

Depending on your age, personality, personal and professional goals, the company for which you work, and where you are in your career journey, you may need to put more or less effort into maintaining a healthy balance. If you're single, relatively young, and have no kids, it can seem almost effortless. On the other hand, if you're forty-five to fifty-five years old, with children at home or in college, and you have aging parents experiencing healthcare issues as they approach the end of life, things will be more complicated. In addition, people in that forty-five to fifty-five age range may feel pressured to work long hours to prove that they still have the mental and physical stamina to compete with the youngsters. For that reason, as an older manager, I've made a big effort to remain nimble, collaborative, open-minded, tech savvy, and astute relative to industry disrupters.

Are there people who have little or no trouble juggling their personal and professional lives? On the surface, it would seem so. That said, appearances can deceive. You can't truly know how easy or difficult it is for someone to maintain a balance without deep insights into their lives and value systems. If someone really enjoys their work, doesn't give a damn about their mental, physical, and spiritual health, and places no value on personal relationships, then the process should be pretty simple: work takes precedence. There's nothing to balance.

Some well-balanced people simply have a gift for time management, or they've developed a knack for it by way of their strategic planning or project management background. These individuals are well-organized, big-picture thinkers who are able to delegate tasks, strike a balance between logic and creativity, and won't hesitate to ask for help from mentors, spiritual counselors, therapists, or friends to identify and manage the interdependent elements of their lives. These people are good at recognizing what they don't know and when it's time to seek assistance from a qualified third party.

For those of us who are not natural-born time managers and whose families are the number one priority, it's important to understand that everything is negotiable and that we have the agency to make choices. Given this understanding, we are very intentional about which roles and responsibilities we accept and how we manage them.

Before saying yes to a promotion or a new assignment, be sure you know what you're saying yes to. Moving up the corporate ladder often means less time for family, so consider carefully before you accept a promotion that may force you to miss most of the milestones in your kids' lives—little league games, piano recitals, school plays, graduations, and so on. Believe it or not, some people *do* turn down career advancement opportunities after deciding that time with the family means more to them than higher compensation and a shiny new title.

Of course, corporate culture is the biggest determinant of how much effort you'll have to devote to juggling life and work. Although some companies encourage employees to lead rich lives by limiting their work schedules and taking vacations, others believe that your mobile device is an extension of the office. These firms will unreasonably expect you to respond to emails, phone calls, and even meetings during nontraditional hours.

Fortunately, a few companies are taking progressive steps to ensure that employees are positioned to achieve a healthy work–life balance. In March 2021, for example, Citigroup CEO Jane Fraser announced to the global workforce that we should make every effort to *not* schedule meetings outside of the normal eight-to-six zone. Going further, she then announced Zoom-free Fridays, meaning no on-camera meetings should be scheduled on Fridays as a way to reduce the amount of Zoom fatigue that occurred after the Covid-19 pandemic.

Unfortunately, internal and external expectations of how hard and long you should work may also depend on your age, race, ethnicity, gender, and sexual orientation. In my experience, African Americans, Latinos, women, and members of the

LGBTQ communities sometimes feel pressured by their superiors (or put a lot of pressure on themselves) to prove that they are as good as (or better than) their straight white male counterparts. Members of these minority groups, as well as some older workers, may work to the point of burnout (or beyond), and they may be reluctant to take time off for fear that if they take a short break, much less a real vacation, they'll lose ground to their competitors. This may seem like paranoia, but sometimes people really *are* out to get you. I once worked with a middle-age supervisor who was reluctant to take any time off. I thought the guy was being dramatic, but sure enough, when he finally did go on a vacation, he was replaced (by me) as manager of the project on which we'd been working. (Note: I never asked to become the project manager.)

The Ultimate Stress Tests

During a typical week, maintaining a healthy work–life balance may not be an issue. You probably won't even think about it. And this state of affairs may well continue for many months or years. But eventually, major life events will catch up with you and begin placing big demands on your time and mental energy—events such as:

- Elder care for parents or other family members
- A job promotion
- Death (especially when the death leaves you as a single parent or forces you—as a grandparent—to become a parent again, or when the death requires you to take in a parent or an in-law who can no longer live alone)

- An unexpected job loss (yours or a loved one's)
- A sudden illness (yours or a loved one's)
- Marriage or divorce
- Financial problems
- Job relocation (yours or that of your spouse)
- Disasters (a house fire, storm, flood)
- Legal problems

One of the greatest challenges that I ever faced happened when I found myself going through a divorce and post-divorce with three children. After settling for joint custody of our daughters, my ex-wife and I initially lived within five miles of each other to ensure an easier transition for the children. Then, my former spouse remarried and moved sixty miles away.

This was grueling because I had an established routine with my children around which I scheduled all my nonessential business travel. This change also lengthened the amount of time (to nearly four hours) needed to pick up and drop off my children at their mother's house between Friday and Sunday. Previously, I'd also spent parts of my weekend catching up on work emails so that I'd be ready to go on Monday mornings. The change threw this routine out of whack.

So, I had to make some adjustments. I had my assistant reduce the number of back-to-back meetings that were scheduled so I'd have time to digest the volume of information that I was required to absorb on a daily basis. I also included my direct reports in more meetings so that they'd be prepared to perform certain tasks in the event I needed to delegate to them. Although my ex-wife's remarriage and move were a challenge, I decided to view the situation as an opportunity to self-reflect—to embrace the fact that when shit happens, we have to find a way to muddle through it.

I also came to appreciate, more than ever, that working sixty to seventy hours a week is not normal or healthy—and in many instances, not necessary. Too often, those extra hours on the job were not appreciated . . . or rewarded at bonus time. During this period, I also came to realize that being a manager did not mean that I had to do every little thing. Others were willing and able to step into the challenges, not because they saw it as a pathway to professional growth but because I had cultivated a team of employees who felt respected and appreciated. Because I valued them, they were more than willing to reciprocate.

Hey, boss, is there anything that I can help you with? Is there anything that I can take off your plate?

I was out to lunch, and because you looked busy, I picked you up something. . . .

Instead of defeating me, this personal challenge allowed me to finally reap the rewards of the collaborative and positive work culture that I had built.

Keep this in mind as you climb the corporate ladder and reach a position where you can influence the company's culture. As much as a toxic work environment can contribute to a poor work–life balance, a positive team-oriented culture can facilitate a healthy work–life balance.

Be aware, also, of how the pressures placed on you, and that you place on yourself, are impacting your personal life and the lives of your colleagues and subordinates. For example, are you afraid of being undermined by an ambitious, unscrupulous subordinate or colleague? Do you worry that a decision detrimental to your authority or career might be made in your absence? If you said yes to either of these, does that make you fearful of taking a vacation or allowing your subordinates to take time off? Do you schedule conference calls during the family dinner or read work emails when the kids are vying for your attention?

A manager who models workaholic behavior can infect the rest of their team (and their children) with that behavior, establishing an unspoken expectation that workaholism is a baseline requirement for good leaders.

In sum, are you perpetuating the problem, or actively working toward a solution?

CHAPTER SEVEN

Feeling Stuck?

I have been driven many times upon my knees by the overwhelming conviction that I had nowhere else to go.

—Abraham Lincoln

You're not alone, Abe.

Sooner or later, many of us reach a crisis point in our careers—a point at which we feel trapped, weighted down by our previous choices.

When that moment arrives, we may suddenly identify with Phil Connors, the cynical weatherman played by Bill Murray in the movie *Groundhog Day*. After it dawns on him that he's trapped in a time loop that forces him to relive the same February 2 over and over, Phil visits a local watering hole and says: "What would you do if you were stuck in one place, and every day was exactly the same, and nothing that you did mattered?"

When the Pursuit of Happiness Reaches a Dead End

I can't explain how Phil Connors came to be trapped in *his* time loop, but I can identify how many of my colleagues and I came to be trapped in *ours*. And I can testify that Phil's attitude toward feeling stuck is very true to life.

I think the main cause of feeling stuck is a sudden, revelatory awareness about all the *sacrifices* that come with being a corporate American—all the trade-offs that we professionals make over the course of our careers. Month after month, year after year, we devote enormous quantities of time, physical energy, and mental energy to performing our duties, fulfilling our responsibilities, and steadily climbing the corporate ladder. It's a huge investment, one that requires a no-looking-back commitment. Once you commit, you spend many precious hours networking, planning, strategizing, and busting your ass to achieve an increasingly ambitious list of goals, *without* taking much time to consider *why* you're doing all of it.

Until . . . one day, you actually take the time to consider *why* you've been doing all of it. And when that happens, you may find yourself asking questions.

- What's the point of all this?
- Is this what I *really* want to be doing?
- Do I want to continue in this direction for another ten, twenty, thirty years?
- Have I sacrificed too much for the sake of my career?
- Am I happy with my life as a whole?
- How do I get out of this mess?

If your answers to such questions are "I don't know" or "Hell no!" you've got a problem. I've been there, and it's not pleasant. When I reached my crisis point, my feelings ping-ponged from numbness, confusion, and frustration to anger and desperation and back again. And my symptoms were relatively mild compared with some of my colleagues'. For example, I recently spoke with a friend who sacrificed much of her personal life to focus on her career. She's only now (decades later) wondering if she did the right thing. She never married, never had children, never put a lot of effort into personal relationships. She literally woke up one morning, realized that the years were rapidly slipping away and that all she had to show for her dedication and sacrifice was her job. Was the job worth all that effort and expense? Was it fulfilling? For many years, she would have instantly said *yes!* Today, she's not so sure.

If you think I'm describing the archetypal midlife crisis, think again. This kind of existential doubt can occur at almost any point in your career. I say "almost" because until the accumulated weight of your work–life choices begins to significantly narrow your options, you're less likely to feel stuck. And if you *do* feel stuck, you should be able to quickly unstick yourself.

Different people will feel stuck for different reasons. Some will feel trapped as soon as their work becomes routine. Others might feel trapped because they see no opportunity for advancement at their current company—and that might be true. Still others will feel trapped because they aren't happy working in a particular industry or following their original career path.

Before you act on your feelings of being stuck, however, it's imperative that you differentiate between what you *feel* and what you *should know*. Are you really trapped, or are you merely unprepared for the next chapter of your life? Would your uneasy feelings disappear if you searched for a new opportunity—the kind that doesn't (usually) land in your lap? Would you feel better if your direct report dropped dead tomorrow morning? Do you have viable options?

Some "sticky" situations can be resolved quite simply. Others are nearly intractable. For example: I had a mentee ("Bianca") who was employed by a Fortune 100 corporation. Bianca loved the company and had worked there for almost ten years. She was consistently ranked as a top performer and poised on the cusp of a promotion.

All was well until a new department manager walked through the door, a manager who, during one of her first business meetings, made some very misinformed (many would say "insulting") comments. Among other things, the manager said that Puerto Ricans were not real Americans. Not only did Bianca find these comments offensive, as well as inaccurate, she believed they put the company at risk, given the nature of their business and the demographics of the employee base.

Although the comments made Bianca cringe, given the racial, social, and political climate of the time, and while some of her colleagues were embarrassed for the manager, she kept her cool. Rather than arguing with her new manager in front of everyone, Bianca decided to wait and seek the wise counsel of trusted advisors within her inner circle. Following this, and in an effort to be a good corporate citizen, she decided to have a nonconfrontational conversation with the manager.

Unfortunately, the nonconfrontation conversation went terribly. Instead of listening to what Bianca had to say or apologizing for causing offense, the manager hit the denial button and became defensive. She refused to acknowledge that she'd said or done anything wrong and was visibly angry after the discussion. This was not the response Bianca was expecting, much less hoping for. From that point forward, the manager was noticeably insecure in Bianca's presence and began treating her as a threat to be eliminated.

Bianca wasn't trying to be a threat. She wasn't gunning for the manager's job or trying to get the person "canceled." On the contrary, she was displaying an admirable level of maturity and leadership. She wanted to be a good team player by not embarrassing the manager in front of her colleagues and subordinates.

But as the saying goes, no good deed goes unpunished, and punishment was exactly what Bianca's manager had in mind. Soon, the manager began casting Bianca as a negative stereotype, labeling her as angry, confrontational, and combative. The manager then wrote her up, which delayed a promised and well-deserved promotion.

Bianca felt stuck.

She *was* stuck.

In theory, Bianca could have taken the matter to her one-up manager, but she didn't. And the reason she didn't is where the plot thickens. Earlier, Bianca's one-up manager had made inappropriate advances toward her—advances she chose not to report. She figured that this guy was not her direct report, which put a buffer (in the form of her previous manager) between him and her. Supportive and nurturing, the previous manager had been a big reason for Bianca's success. In addition, Bianca didn't want to be perceived as a snitch. Therefore, she felt she'd be unable to rely on any impartial support from the one-up.

Couldn't Bianca have gone to HR to resolve the issue? Surely, the HR department of a Fortune 100 must have policies, procedures, and guidelines in place to help people in Bianca's position or (at the very least) a whistleblower hotline. Well, yes, she could have. However, although Bianca loved the company and her job, she didn't trust the system that had been implemented to protect her from harm. She didn't believe her complaint would be anonymous, nor did she believe that HR personnel would competently resolve the situation.

(If you're wondering how someone could love a company, but not trust it to protect her from wrongdoing, consider this: Like tens of thousands of African Americans, my grandfather served in the armed forces during World War II. He loved his country. At the same time, Black service members didn't trust that the system would protect them from some of their fellow citizens because, during that era, it didn't protect them. So they loved America while simultaneously recognizing its flaws and hoping that, someday, things would get better. This is very much how Bianca felt about her company.)

Why didn't she simply transfer to another department? Two reasons:

1. She had a specialized job with specialized skills that were specific to that department.
2. Company policy prohibited employees from receiving transfers or promotions if they were in the midst of a

corrective action plan, which is where Bianca sat at the time. (The manager's report triggered a corrective action plan.)

If you'd been in Bianca's shoes, what would you have done? Your boss is a vengeful asshole bent on ruining your career; your boss's boss is a sexual predator. You can't transfer or get promoted to another department, and you don't trust the system to resolve the situation in your favor. Would you have chosen the "nuclear option" and quit your job?

At first glance, that seems like the only logical recourse, but keep in mind something that I mentioned earlier: certain companies break your compensation into three buckets: (1) base salary, (2) short-term incentive (annual bonus), and (3) long-term incentive plan (paid out over several years). Bianca's firm was just such a company, so if she'd have walked away before her LTIP vested, she would have forfeited a significant amount of money.

"I also didn't want to be the girl who snitched, and cost someone their job," she said. "At the end of the day, I sucked it up and, while I felt violated, I was not physically hurt.

"I feel stuck because I battle with my visual appearance and speech. I'm multiracial, so my hair is naturally curly, but I wear it straight so I can blend in and make the masses feel comfortable. I know I'm a better bet for promotion when I maintain a certain appearance, so as a Latina woman who identifies as biracial, bringing my authentic self to the table was not an option. I had to identify that imaginary line and how close that I could come to it. But crossing that line wasn't going to happen."

Finding yourself in a toxic work environment—or in Bianca's case, a *hostile* work environment—is one of the worst-case scenarios you can encounter. More often, people feel trapped for lesser reasons. Regardless of why you feel stuck, it's important to prepare an escape plan—one that's instantly ready to implement. That means making sure that you update your résumé regularly, along with your LinkedIn profile; that you keep your professional network active; that you have six months' worth of living expenses in a savings account; and that you continually arrange external job interviews to gauge your worth in the current job market.

Even if your hands seem tied with golden handcuffs, don't give up. If you decide to move on from your current job and move to another organization, you *can* negotiate with a prospective employer to make you whole again, either through a sign-on bonus, the base pay, or shares of the new company's stock on a vesting schedule similar to what you're leaving behind. Remember, many things *are* negotiable, even when the employer says (at first) that they're not.

Another option is to launch your own business. This was the path taken by a former employee, Abdullah Sheikh. Born in Somalia, Abdullah earned an undergraduate degree from the University of Saudi Arabia before coming to the United States as a political refugee. I met Abdullah in the mid-2000s when he was a member of my banking support operations team. Abdullah was a hard worker but also very complacent: he was just happy to be safe and to provide for his family. Even though his career was stuck in second gear, he wasn't especially concerned about it—not at first. One day, however, he overheard me asking some employees why they weren't taking advantage of the firm's tuition reimbursement program. At that moment, a light bulb went off in his head, and he decided to leverage that benefit. First, he went back to school and obtained his master's degree. Then, he began preparing a business plan for his own company. Then, he resigned from the bank. Today, he owns and operates a business that grosses $5 million annually.

Another acquaintance ("Julia") pursued a similar path in order to become unstuck from a racist and sexist work environment.

After studying accounting as an undergraduate, Julia joined the Atlanta office of a Big Four consulting firm on a prestigious, high-profile account. "I was the Black poster girl, being heralded in all of their marketing materials and representing the firm in their diversity recruiting. After joining that project, I quickly discovered that there were two career paths: continue working eighty hours a week supporting the project for my company, or go work for the client.

"My boss on that job was racist and sexist, and each and every one of those eighty hours per week was absolutely hell. At the time, I thought, 'This *has* to be an anomaly. This can't be what corporate America is supposed to be about.' He would make sexist comments if I took my purse to the bathroom, such as: 'Oh, you must be on your period.' Another time, I excused myself to take a call from my mother, and he asked me what she did for a living. I said that she was a superintendent. He looked at the other white men in the room, and said, 'She must be using the fancier term for janitor.' I was infuriated but had to keep my composure out of fear of being labeled emotional, so I said calmly, 'My mother is not a janitor; she's the superintendent of a school district.'

"This racist and sexist behavior occurred all day, every day, and to make matters worse, the project team was working out of a very small, confined space. I was the only woman, the only person of color, and just twenty-one years old. I'm not sure what could have prepared me for what I was dealing with, because it was exhausting. That was on top of carrying all the boxes, carrying all the bags, ordering lunch, getting coffee, etcetera. I felt like the corporate version of Kizzy [from *Roots*]. It was degrading."

One day, Julia ran into a female partner she knew, who mentioned that she was about to launch a joint venture. "The partner asked if I'd be interested in joining the group. I told her that I'd love to, but that I was currently working on the X Project. The partner grimaced, knowing it was very difficult to get on or off that project. 'Let me see what I can do,' the partner said. But she pulled some strings and got me into the group. She then said, 'I'll put you in charge of REITs (real estate investment trusts),' which were new at the time. My response was, 'That sounds fine. I'll see you on Monday.' I then rushed to Barnes & Noble to buy every book I could find on REITs because I didn't know a thing about real estate.

"Fast-forward to today, and I'm chief operating officer of a retail, grocery, and shopping center REIT. And I got here because I was running away from the abusive racist and sexist culture of that consulting firm. That female partner could have been starting a group developing slime, and I would have volunteered. Since then, I've created a name for myself developing mixed-use development platforms for a number of very recognizable projects."

Julia was smart. First, she leveraged the partner's clout to ensure she could make a clean break from the project. Second, she had the partner frame her request for Julia as a specific talent need. By doing so, Julia avoided political blowback because the escape *did not appear* to be an escape. If the perception had been that Julia was running away, the good ole boys network would have controlled the narrative. They could have labeled her as someone who was simply not up for the job on the X Project. Fortunately, the female partner knew the players and understood the politics. She knew that running away from that project would have been career suicide for Julia, so her positioning of Julia's transfer helped preserve—and then advance—Julia's career prospects.

Your Job (Probably) Won't Be Totally Fulfilling

I've met people who feel *perpetually* trapped and are resigned to feeling that way. For them, work *is* suffering. A job isn't meant to be fun, rewarding, or fulfilling. A job is a cross that we must bear until the merciful hand of retirement (or death) releases us from its sterile grip. Life *can* be beautiful, but work is not. It's tedious and dreary.

Conversely, I've also known people who have never felt stuck. For them, work is bliss. They can't imagine a world without their jobs. Retirement would be a living death. One friend's grandfather was so happy with his job behind the butcher counter at a grocery store, which he owned with his brother, he was rarely seen at home during daylight hours. (Rumor had it that he was trying to avoid his wife and kids, not that he was a vampire.) I don't believe most of these people will ever feel stuck because that would imply that they want more from life than a job. How do you miss something you don't desire or dream about?

The rest of us fall somewhere between these two extremes. We like our jobs—or parts of them—but we also relish our free time, our personal relationships, and our outside interests.

Most of us, most of the time, will not feel trapped in go-nowhere jobs, and on our deathbeds, we won't lament the sacrifices we made to advance up the corporate ladder. But there will be times when many of us feel trapped, especially if we land in a work environment where we're abused or we believe that we aren't being fairly compensated for our contributions or that we're being passed over for promotions or that we have no options for improving our situation. If you're feeling stuck, the first—and most important—step is to determine the root cause. Ask yourself these questions to determine why you're feeling this way:

- How did I get here?
- Where am I today versus where I thought I would be?
- Where am I today versus where I *should* be, given my true potential?
- Am I trapped in a job that I don't like or an entire career that I don't like?
- Is it the *job* that I dislike, or is it the company, the culture, or certain people (e.g., one or more of my supervisors)?
- What actions could I take right now that would improve my situation? (Start with the least radical actions, and work your way up—if necessary.)
- Which activities and pursuits (personal and professional) do I find most fulfilling, and what steps could I take to increase the time I spend on these activities/pursuits? Could I turn one or more of these activities/pursuits into a career?
- Who can I turn to for advice on getting unstuck—people who will tell me what I need to hear, not just what I want to hear? (Don't discount the services of a good therapist.)

▪ If I had to trade money for career fulfillment, which would I choose?

Look inward and ask, "Have I executed on my plan? Have I done everything necessary to be successful?" These last two questions will help determine whether the problem is you or "them."

But whatever the root cause, you need to realize that the birdcage is open. Wide open. Very few people are truly trapped.

When I arrived at my crisis point, I recognized it immediately. I realized that I'd reached an inflection point in my life. I also realized that I needed to pause, take a step back, and assess my situation in a very analytical manner. After all, I had an MBA. I was being paid to develop comprehensive solutions for complex global organizations. But over the years, I was conditioned to focus on the problems of *others*. I was not conditioned to think about my needs and how to address them from a practical business perspective. Eventually, I concluded that my crisis was as much an opportunity as a dilemma. It was an opportunity for me to develop and execute a business plan to improve my life.

Then and there, I decided to blaze my own trail—to focus on achieving my own goals based on my own success criteria, not those of corporate America or society in general. This decision led me to a new level of freedom. If at times my corporate career became totally unbearable due to the toxicity of the environment, boredom, or the like, I would pursue other opportunities that could provide satisfaction, for example, as an art investor and gallerist, a photographer/artist, and a community activist. Focusing on these interests allowed me to shift my focus to the areas that were (and are) fulfilling.

Most of us will not find total fulfillment through our work for the simple reason that most jobs are not designed to be fulfilling. If you look up the dictionary definition of *job*, you'll find entries such as "a piece of work, especially a specific task done as part of the routine of one's occupation or for an agreed price" (Dictionary.com) and "a regular remunerative position" (*Webster's*). These definitions strongly suggest that jobs were never intended as self-actualization machines.

I've long known that a job could never fulfill all my intellectual and emotional needs because my life comprises too many different dimensions. No one job could fulfill every one of my mental, spiritual, and creative needs, and I'm okay with that. Although I gain a great deal of satisfaction from my work, my primary reason for working is to finance my external responsibilities, interests, and passions.

On the other hand, if someone's identity is tied to their job—if everything that matters most to them is intertwined with work—what happens if that job disappears? Do they cease to exist as unique individuals? For some people, sadly, the answer is yes.

When all you have is your job, but one day you come to the realization that everything you've been working toward—the recognition, compensation, benefits, and career growth—is capped, you may well experience a mental meltdown. You may feel like you've reached the end of the road, with no detour signs in sight.

Today's parents are fond of telling their children that "there are no limits to what you can achieve." That's not true. Although every child has the potential to achieve great things, there are limits to what can be done. Simply because our time on earth is limited, few of us will achieve *everything* we set out to do. And it's when this realization strikes that many a career crisis begins.

We have to be okay with the fact that time is limited and that we may not fulfill all our dreams. We have to be okay with the fact that we'll achieve some goals and not others. We have to cut ourselves some slack and view ourselves as the rock stars we are for having accomplished what we have. If you need a fresh perspective, solicit opinions and advice from people you respect. Get their thoughts on where you are and how you can move forward. Be sure to talk with people who will give it to you straight, not people who will yes you to death.

Also: Take a moment, once a day or once a week, to appreciate who you are, what you've done, and all the obstacles that you've overcome to reach your current level of success. Just as important, let go of any fear of moving forward. As Robert DeNiro tells Al Pacino in the movie *Heat*, "Never get involved in a relationship that you can't get away from when you feel the Heat coming around the corner." There will be times when moving forward requires you to walk away from certain people and organizations. Otherwise, the "Heat" will hold you back. Better to step into the unknown, by switching jobs or careers, than stagnate. Fear of the unknown is a career killer. Yet some people are so afraid of change that they'd rather stick with a dead-end job than walk away from old relationships.

When he was twenty years old, a friend of mine (a journalism major at NYU) landed an entry-level job at the *New York Times* while he was still in his junior year. He'd spent years aspiring to work for the newspaper of record, and never thought he'd get a job there until much later in his career. A couple of years on, however, after learning that the vast majority of reporters and editors were hired from the outside (promotions from copyboy to reporter were very rare), he began looking for work elsewhere. It was an agonizing decision because, in his mind, there was no place to go but down. There was no newspaper more prestigious than the *New York Times*.

Still, my friend swallowed his fear and found a job elsewhere. Today, he has no regrets about leaving, though he has yet to achieve everything he set out to accomplish when he was a college student. Some of his peers, however, couldn't overcome their fears. They stuck with the entry-level jobs well into their thirties—not a good way to "fast track" a career.

Find Your Passion(s)

One day you will wake up and there won't be any more time to do the things you've always wanted to do. Do it now.
—Paulo Coelho, *The Alchemist*

Nothing I've written should be interpreted to mean that prioritizing your career is "unhealthy" or that it's weird to be passionate about your job. For some people, a job is not just a way to make ends meet but also a lifelong mission to make a positive difference in the world. For others, work is about living their dream by putting their knowledge and degrees to good use. If you're one of these people, kudos! It's important to recognize, though, that your attitude may evolve as you enter different phases of life.

Personally, I take pride in having the kind of job I do because, in many ways, I am the fulfillment of my ancestors' dreams. This doesn't erase all the difficulties and headaches that I experience on a day-to-day basis, but it helps. My work is especially fulfilling on those days when I'm able to effect positive change or make things better for others. My life's mission is to be a humane leader and leave a legacy of future leaders, depositing more into society than I withdraw. That being said, there *have* been times when my work and workplace culture have literally made me sick to my stomach. (I developed an ulcer earlier in my career.) On those days, I remind myself that sometimes you have to do what's necessary to do what you love.

I also remind myself that all of us stand on the shoulders of giants, and furthering their legacy is a part of our own fulfillment. You can never pay back the sacrifices of your forebears, but you can be a model of excellence. You can be someone who makes your family proud and who inspires future generations. Happiness and fulfillment are things that everyone feeds off. Sometimes, just doing our jobs well makes us examples that will inspire others and ourselves. This world is in desperate need of inspiration, so don't lose sight of the big picture. Don't lose sight of what *really* matters.

These sentiments may seem trite to those of you who are in your twenties and thirties, but once you get a little older, and start thinking about the epitaph you might want on your tombstone, your attitude could shift in a hurry.

I've also been fortunate in that I've always found reasons to live besides my job, and it's a good bet that many of you have also discovered interests, activities, and causes that inject more color, excitement, and meaning into your life.

How do you know that you're not simply distracting yourself with meaningless pastimes? First, there's nothing wrong with a few meaningless pastimes. Second, you'll know you've uncovered nonwork reasons for living when you find yourself investing more and more of your time, talent, and treasure into things that excite your emotions and imagination. Things that cause little bursts of adrenaline to course through your veins. It doesn't matter whether society considers these pursuits to be righteous world-changing causes or mindless hobbies. What matters is that you're passionate about them and would continue to be passionate about them if you lost your job tomorrow.

I've worked with people who were passionate about politics. During election season, they maxed out on campaign donations and used their vacation time to canvass in battleground states. I've also had colleagues who used their personal time and resources to go on mission trips in service to others, and they would do this each and every year. And I've worked with senior financial executives who fulfill their passion for music by performing in public. Carla Harris, vice chair of Morgan Stanley, is a singer who's appeared at Carnegie Hall. That's one hell of hobby.

My situation was a little different from most corporate Americans'. I was an artist before I was a financial services professional. When I was in my twenties, I worked as a fashion and celebrity photographer, publishing my work under the pseudonym Yusuf Rashad. It was banking and financial services that were my "outside" passion. They provided me with the extra challenge of working in a space that was exciting, new, and (eventually) relatively lucrative. Before I went into financial services full-time, I was simply applying my transferable skills from the art world to the corporate world, with the aim of picking up a few business skills for use in my photography career.

How do you balance the pursuit of your outside passions with your job? Well, when I was much younger, I proudly subscribed to the rule of 168. There are 168 hours in a week, so my thinking was: "It's up to me to decide how I want to use those hours to accomplish the things that are important to me." My main sacrifice was sleep. I became very comfortable functioning on four to six hours of sleep. I don't recommend this for everyone, but it worked for me.

If you're truly passionate about something, you'll find a way to make time for it while continuing to pay the bills. The key is to never allow your passion for the things you love to dissipate out of sheer neglect. I carried a camera around with me during high school, and I kept at it. I never stopped loving art and eventually opened Renaissance Fine Art Gallery and later the Curtiss Jacobs Gallery while working as an executive for a global financial services firm.

Malaise Prevention

After reaching Mexico in 1519, the conquistador Hernán Cortés ordered his ships to be burned. Although many people assume that Cortés was "motivating" his men by forcing them into a "do or die" situation, his real purpose was to prevent (another attempt at) mutiny—to prevent the crew from packing up the supplies and sailing back to Cuba. Regardless of his intent, the result was the same: there was no option but to conquer the Aztecs or die trying.

Now please understand that I am not a fan of Hernán Cortés or the conquistadors, but the reason I'm referencing this historical nugget about the tragic and brutal slaughter of the Aztecs is because, earlier in this chapter, I said that building a successful career requires a "no-looking-back commitment." That's true. Once you commit to a career, it's important to stay focused on the prize and avoid second-guessing. But there's a world of difference between second-guessing yourself and burning every other option to ashes.

The best way to avoid feeling stuck in a career or job is by reducing the odds of ever *getting* stuck. And the best way to do this is, as mentioned, by keeping your options open: maintain a healthy network of personal and professional contacts, keep your résumé updated, go on job interviews to gauge the current market for your skills and knowledge, and pursue outside interests that will keep you sane when the going gets rough in the office.

Don't place all of your eggs in one basket. Balance is the key to life, and maintaining a good balance means allowing yourself choices in case you need to pivot.

If you don't keep your résumé updated, test the market, and maintain a fully functioning network, you won't be prepared for the unexpected. If a worst-case scenario should arise—you lose your job, your manager is replaced by an asshole, your company merges with a cut-throat-culture company—you'll be stuck for a considerable period. You won't be ready to leap into a new role, move to a different company, or launch a start-up business of your own.

Keep looking ahead, but don't burn the forest down behind you.

Talks about Switching Career Tracks

Bill Stephney is a musician who received a scholarship to Adelphi University on Long Island. Later, after meeting Rick Rubin (a cofounder of Def Jam Records who later became co-president of Columbia Records), Bill was offered a position at Def Jam. At twenty-four, he played a crucial role at Def Jam when the label came to prominence, thanks to acts that included LL Cool J, Public Enemy, the Beastie Boys, and Slick Rick.

"At that point, we were on cruise control, and while I wouldn't necessarily say I was stuck, I would certainly say I was challenged. This was the late eighties, heading into the nineties, a period when many African Americans were revisiting the messages of Malcolm X, which were self-determination and construction of the community. I was working as an employee—a high-profile employee, but still an employee—and was no longer satisfied. I was asking myself, 'Shouldn't I be out there like Russell (Simmons) and Andre (Harrell), establishing my own business?'"

Bill left Def Jam and became an entrepreneur, moving on to run joint ventures with Warner Brothers, Interscope, and Universal Music.

"Now here's where I think I literally got stuck. Around 2000, Napster emerges on the scene and disrupts the music industry like a tsunami. To be frank, the music industry still hasn't figured it out." Music was now free, and the major labels were subdivisions of other businesses that made their money elsewhere. But for independent labels, which made money purely from record sales, the path to survival was narrow: either create music that glorified the drug game or gangster life or demeaned women, which was enveloping the hip-hop music industry, or discover an as yet unknown path.

For Bill, discovering that unknown path was the only option. "I didn't believe in that lifestyle, nor did I want to promote music that fed that energy. I had to remain true to my core set of values. So now I'm stuck because my labels certainly couldn't compete with the labels that were producing the genre that was dominating the industry."

He took an inventory of his skills, relationships, and experiences and decided to leverage his reputation to launch a consultancy with the likes of Viacom, Time Warner, USA Network, and ESPN, among others.

His key message: "Believe in yourself and your past success, because the key to science is replication, which means that if I was able I to grow a business from inception to an industry powerhouse like Def Jam, that means I can do it again in a different environment, industry, or sector."

CHAPTER EIGHT

Recognizing the "Isms"

T*he most blatant instance of racism* that I ever experienced in the workplace occurred at Merrill Lynch. It was early in my corporate career, and I was working the overnight shift in the support services department. Back then, the graphics, print services, desktop publishing, proofing, and copyediting personnel worked together closely to provide support for the investment bankers, who were primarily junior-level employees, that is, first-year analysts or associates.

One night, a woman from the London office burst into the department and demanded that we bump her project to the head of the queue. She was told that we were extremely busy, thanks to a number of rush projects, but that we'd do our best to accommodate her. This, to put it mildly, displeased her. She shouted all the usual reasons for why her project was a top priority, but there was nothing we could do. Eventually, she left.

Two hours before her project was scheduled to be finished, however, she returned to ask how much longer she'd have to wait. She was given the same timeline and told that if we were able to finish early, we'd give her a call. In response, the young woman became enraged. I explained that we were nearing the boundary of our equipment's capabilities, but this wasn't what she wanted to hear. She stormed out.

We ended up beating the timeline by thirty minutes, but instead of displaying any gratitude, she grabbed her materials and shouted: "You slow-ass niggers!"

In retrospect, the scene was a bit comical—a petite, hundred-pound white woman screaming something like that to six men of color. But at the time, everything seemed to unfold in slow motion. I couldn't believe it. Many of us had grown up in "the hood" or in close proximity, and we'd seen (or heard about) bad things happening to people for saying far less.

Then it dawned on me: She viewed us as *servants*—as inferiors. Because of our color and our status as support services workers, we were members of a lower caste who were expected to bow and scrape before her awesome majesty. It reminded me of when I was a recruit in the New York State Police Academy and one of the drill sergeants explained our status as new recruits. The sergeant raised both fists in the air, holding one of them about a foot higher than the other. He said (referring to the higher fist), "This is whale shit." Then (nodding to the lower fist), "And this is you all—until you graduate from the academy."

To our visitor from London, we were lower than whale shit.

The second most egregious incident occurred years later while I was visiting my staff in Asia. I was the global leader, and my staff had a matrix reporting line to the regional leader, an expatriate, or ex-pat. After arriving at the office, I had a traditional face-to-face with this regional leader, during which I asked about a new hire. I then asked if he could direct me to the man's work area and describe his appearance. (I'd communicated with this employee by email and phone, but I'd never seen him.) The regional manager replied, "Describe him? I don't know how to describe him. He's Asian. He looks like an ape, I guess."

I stared at him in shock. How do you respond to a racial slur like that?

I didn't. Instead, I excused myself and went looking for the new employee. Later, I canceled the lunch that I'd scheduled with this manager.

It *Can* Happen Here

If you think the "isms"—racism, sexism, classism, and nepotism—are vestiges of a bygone era, or that discrimination based on these isms has been banished from the meritocratic halls of corporate America, think again.

Although the isms tend to be less overt today than in the decades-old incidents above, racism, sexism, classism, and nepotism continue to pervade American society and, thus, corporate society. Because racism, sexism, and so forth usually manifest in more subtle ways than they once did, many people assume (or desperately want to assume) that they've been eradicated. I wish I could say this were true, but there is far too much evidence—anecdotal and empirical—to the contrary. The numbers don't lie:

- Sixty-nine percent of Black, 53 percent of Asian, and 45 percent of white employees have witnessed a racist incident at work. Another 25 percent stated that they have witnessed other subtle forms of racism that they felt was not significant enough to report.[11]

- In the history of the Fortune 500 list, first published in 1955, there have been only 19 Black CEOs out of 1,800 chief executives.[12]

- Corporate America's top ranks look nothing like the country they serve. Less than 2 percent of top executives at the fifty largest U.S. companies are Black.[13]

- For every 100 men promoted to manager, only 85 women were promoted. This gap was even larger for some women: only 58 Black women and 71 Latinas were promoted. As a result, women remained significantly outnumbered by men in entry-level management at the beginning of 2020. They held just 38 percent of manager-level positions, while men held 62 percent.[14]

- Seventy-two percent of the leadership pipeline beginning with managers is focused on white employees, according to a 2019 McKinsey and Co. study titled "Representation in the Corporate Pipeline by Gender and Race":

  - Entry-level: 65 percent white (35 percent men, 30 percent women)

  - Manager: 72 percent white (45 percent men, 27 percent women)

  - Senior manager/director: 76 percent white (51 percent men, 26 percent women)

  - Vice president: 81 percent white (57 percent men, 24 percent women)

  - Senior vice president: 85 percent white (64 percent men, 21 percent women)

- ⬧ C-suite: 86 percent white (68 percent men, 18 percent women)
- ⬧ One in five C-suite executives is a woman, and only one in twenty-five C-suite executives is a woman of color.[15]
- ▪ For the period from 2017 to 2019:
  - ⬧ Black men earned 87 cents for every dollar a white man earned.
  - ⬧ Hispanic men earned 91 cents for every dollar earned by white men.
  - ⬧ Black workers with bachelor's degrees earned 82 percent of what their white colleagues earned.
  - ⬧ Hispanic workers with bachelor's degrees earned 77 percent of what their white colleagues earned.
  - ⬧ Black workers with advanced degrees earned 71 percent of what their white colleagues earned.
  - ⬧ Hispanic workers with advanced degrees earned 61 percent of what their white colleagues earned.[16]

One can argue that such disparities are the lingering results of historic discrimination, and that these historic injustices take time to remedy. Unfortunately, we've been hearing that "these things take time" for upward of sixty years. By comparison, consider just a few other challenges that corporate America has overcome in far less time:

- ▪ Block chain
- ▪ Cloud computing
- ▪ Electric cars
- ▪ Civilians in space

- e-Commerce
- Three effective Covid-19 vaccines (in less than a year)

Do we believe U.S. companies are capable of overcoming these challenges in a matter of years (or months) but are helpless to create a corporate environment that is consistently fair, equitable, and just? I don't think so. In my view, if fixing the isms were a priority for corporate America, the vast majority of companies would have already fixed the problem.

I once worked for a company that managed to safely unwind tens of billions of dollars in credit default swaps, but "figuring out" how to equitably hire, promote, and compensate their diverse employee population? Apparently, this was too great a challenge.

Or was it?

If the old adage, "Where there's a will, there's a way," holds true, then my former company either didn't want to prioritize the effort or didn't care to address the issue. Either way, there simply wasn't enough *will*.

Depending on whom you talk with, the reasons for this lack of will are attributable to one (or more) of the following:

1. **Conscious** racism, sexism, etcetera, on the part of the majority population (i.e., white men) and/or a belief that the status quo is "the natural order of things."

2. **Unconscious** racism, sexism, etcetera, on the part of the majority population. In other words, many white, male executives have been so inculcated with "ism" values, behaviors, and viewpoints that they exhibit discriminatory behavior without even recognizing that they're doing

it—sometimes in spite of their conscious efforts to be fair and unbiased.

3. **Systemic** racism, sexism, etcetera. Because the isms were stitched into the legal, economic, and social fabric of the United States, with discriminatory institutions, legal codes, and societal norms constructed and maintained over the course of generations, white men who merely approach "business as usual" are unconsciously perpetuating discrimination.

How much weight you assign each explanation depends, of course, on your race, sex, socioeconomic status, and personal experiences. For example, it should come as no surprise that my friend Julia (see Chapter 7) leans toward the first explanation, given her traumatic experiences at the Big Four consulting firm in Atlanta. For my part, I lean toward explanations 2 and 3.

In my view, everyone's values, behaviors, and views are shaped by many influences from a very young age. We're aware of some of these influences, and not of others. One of the influences that we're least aware of, but one that profoundly affects us, is the culture in which we live. If the typical middle-class white male comes of age in a society—and a work culture—dominated by men who look and talk like him and who share similar backgrounds, he will probably come to view this as the "normal" state of affairs. Even when the society pays lip service to equality and fairness, this man is still swimming in a pond that was built during previous eras—eras when racism, sexism, and segregation were considered normal (or even positive). I think this last explanation helps us better understand why—and how—discrimination continues to thrive. Even if the average white male executive is personally repulsed by the isms, and consciously wants to create a more just and fair corporate culture, he has been conditioned to feel comfortable with the status quo—a status quo that works to his benefit.

Interestingly, it would appear that while the status quo benefits white males, it is not benefiting the organizations for which they work. A few more facts for your consideration:

- Diverse companies enjoy 2.3 times higher cash flow per employee.
- Forty-three percent of companies with diverse boards noticed higher profits.
- Racially and ethnically diverse companies are 35 percent more likely to perform better.[17]

Because the majority population has inherited a system that continues to exclude historically marginalized people, simply going about business as usual helps to maintain a discriminatory system. To eradicate the isms, the system itself must be profoundly reformed or completely overturned. To accomplish this, however, we must learn how to recognize the subtle forms that the isms now take and identify the mechanisms by which the current system is automatically perpetuated. The fact that senior leader after senior leader is absolutely fine with talking about the importance of a diverse workforce but then continuously publishes an organizational chart with photos of their racially homogeneous team of direct reports is absolutely insulting, and disgraceful.

The Subtle Ways in Which Isms Manifest

For members of the majority population, it may seem that racism and sexism have gone underground. Many white men may not even hear the "dog whistles" used today. However, as an African American, the ways in which the isms now manifest aren't particularly "subtle" to me.

For example: On many occasions, I've participated in roundtable discussions during which we "stack rank" employees. (This is a practice in which managers rank employees on a curve according to their performance.) Time and again, underperforming men were ranked higher than they should have been or were spared from termination thanks to rationalizations such as "he's going through a divorce" or "he just bought a new house" or "his kids are in private school" or "his wife doesn't work." None of these reasons has anything to do with performance.

Some of these rationalizations are at least as old as me. In an episode of the *Mary Tyler Moore Show* broadcast in 1972, Moore's character, Mary Richards, learns that she's being paid less than the male employee who previously had her job. She decides to confront her boss, Mr. Grant (Ed Asner), about the discrepancy, but is quickly shot down:

MARY: Let me get this straight. The only reason he was paid more than I am is because he was a man?

MR. GRANT: Oh sure, it has nothing to do with your work.

MARY: No, no, wait a minute, because I want to understand this. I'm doing as good a job as he did.

MR. GRANT: Better!

MARY: Better! And I'm being paid less because—

MR. GRANT: You're a woman.

MARY: Well, Mr. Grant, there is no good reason why two people doing the same job, at the same place, shouldn't be making the—

MR. GRANT: He had a family to support. You don't. Now why don't you come back when you have an answer to that?[18]

Here's the answer to that: Some of my female colleagues were the breadwinners in their homes. Some had spouses who suffered from debilitating ailments. Some were funding their children's private school educations. But I never *once* heard a male colleague justify a woman's performance issues with the excuses given for the men. In fact, these men were more likely to find fault with women for no good reason. For example, a former manager once said to me about a female colleague, "I'm not sure how serious she is about her career. She's out a lot." The reason she was "out a lot" is because she'd been on maternity leave.

This lack of support from male managers and colleagues, especially when it comes to advancing or protecting their careers, is one of the most common forms that sexism takes today. Just ask my former mentee Christina Lucas, now president of Envista Forensics.

"I did three ex-pat assignments [Brazil, Japan, and Bulgaria], and not once did I receive the safe landing that many of my other colleagues received upon their return to the States. When I returned Stateside from Brazil, there was no role for me. Upon returning from Japan, where I had to clean up the mess that a former colleague had left, my role was eliminated and, in order to maintain employment with the firm, I had to accept a demotion." To add insult to injury, the employee whose mess she cleaned up returned to a promotion.

Sometimes, Christina discovered that discrimination was far from subtle. While living in Brazil, for example, she saw both colorism and racism. "I went to Brazil as an ex-pat, and the company treated me as if I were a local employee. I received very few perks that most ex-pats received, and I had no engagements with multinationals. I was left to work with a domestic client base, where few if any of the clients communicated in my native English or Spanish (in which I have a level of fluency). I was the lead of the onsite team, yet clients would frequently ask me to get them coffee, or ask me to take notes, rarely ever recognizing me as the manager of the team.

"It was very difficult to build social or political capital with the good ole boys club," she added. "I felt no allegiance or loyalty to them, because none was shown to me." The exception occurred in Japan, where the local administrative assistants, having observed the inconsistencies in the treatment of Christina, did little things to shield her from bad behavior, like making sure she was never seated, on trains or planes, next to male executives with "roving eyes." Knowing that Christina had no network or support base, the secretaries would occasionally invite her out after work or on the weekends. "They proactively created a community to support me in the spirit of sisterhood, which was a bit of a silver lining."

With regard to racism, the "dog whistles" can sometimes sound more like sirens. For example, early in my managerial career, an HR manager worried that I may have been hiring too many Hispanic men. I was taken aback, totally perplexed by this assertion. At first, I thought the HR manager was implying that I had a homosexual attraction to Latino men and that my hiring decisions were based on sexual desire. In reality, I was a new manager, with limited training, experience, or support, and I hadn't been given a formal process to follow. As the volume of work exploded, one of my star employees would simply come to me and say, "I have a friend looking for a job. I'd be more than willing to train him on the production equipment if you give him a chance." So I'd interview these referrals, and if they checked out, I hired them. This created a pipeline of new employees for lower-level, get-your-foot-in-the-door types of roles. I never worried that I was hiring too many Latino men, and not enough African Americans, white men, or women of any color. I didn't think about the racial and gender balance because I was an African American hiring non–African Americans.

However, from that point on, I made it my business to be consciously aware of the environments that I was creating. And as I advanced in my career, I would share a version of that story with employees I promoted into the managerial ranks so that they would be conscious about their hiring choices and reponsibilities.

Of course, sometimes a dog whistle is exactly that. All too often, managers and HR people will express "concern" about the intelligence, communication skills, and educational credentials of the Black candidates—and *only* the Black candidates.

"I once worked in a Diversity and Inclusion leadership role at a particular firm, and whenever I spoke with my manager about a Black employee, she would allude to their intelligence," said Chris Michel, who is now a chief diversity officer. "She never did that when she was referring to anyone else, and that raised two important points: first, I wondered how she referred to me when I was not around; second, I began to see that *this* [focus on intelligence] was probably the reason we didn't see Black talent breaking through those glass barriers. If this senior HR leader speaks in this unfiltered way in front of me about employees for whom I'm trying to ensure a fair and just career path . . . then perhaps this is the prevailing view of the executive leadership team that makes hiring and promotion decisions. If so, then it's fairly evident that no Black employee will have any success breaking through. It appears that they all have this bias about our intellectual capacity.

"This happened so frequently that I finally pointed it out to her. Her response was that she didn't mean it 'that way.' So I asked myself, 'Well, what way *did* you mean it?' The sad thing is she wasn't even cognizant of what she was saying and to whom she was expressing these views. She and the executive leadership team seemed unaware that these attitudes kept them from recognizing the organizational talent that they claimed to value so deeply. This experience, among others, made it crystal clear to me that existence of a true meritocracy is the biggest bunch of BS that anyone has ever foisted upon any workplace. Obviously, you have to produce, but in some instances, that's not even a criterion. Many people consistently fail up because [success] is all about their relationships."

Here are other common forms in which the isms subtly manifest:

- Excessive criticism of employees who belong to historically marginalized groups, as well as frequent second-guessing of their judgment, competence, and abilities

- Asking inappropriate questions about family background during interviews
- Refusing to make eye contact with women and/or employees of color
- Referencing stereotypes during conversations, in meetings, or in email communications
- Demonstrating a pattern of excluding certain employees from professional or social events
- Demonstrating a pattern of excluding certain employees from special projects, stretch assignments and other growth opportunities—the types that lead to promotions
- Non-performance-based rationalizations for why female and/or minority candidates should not, or cannot, be hired or promoted

Regarding that last bullet point, Rahsan Boykin, General Counsel of the Hashflow Foundation a blockchain startup and former I/ML lead within Google's legal team, recalled several occasions during his career where creative and not-so-creative rationalizations were deployed to justify blatant sexism: "Earlier in my career, before i joined Google, I worked for companies that supported sales teams. I've been on sales calls where executives told me that they did not want a woman or religious person as a part of their team because they knew the sales teams occasionally took clients to strip clubs. I was also in an executive meeting where I made the argument that a woman should be added to the board of directors, thinking it would be a noncontroversial statement. Needless to say, it was a huge controversial statement. I received significant pushback from an executive who expressed a concern that they shouldn't bring on a woman because a woman might bring a charge of sexual harassment. I was astonished. Another was making excuses about how he just didn't know how they could bring a woman on because he had no women in his professional. While they were volleying excuses back and forth, I sat there thinking, "We have a long way to go."

I left the conversation thinking, "I find it amazing that in your combined decades of business experience across multiple industries here and abroad, you don't believe you can find one qualified woman to sit on the board with you. Off of the top of my head, I can think of eight." I was embarrassed for them.

The Insidious Interaction of Isms

Although classism and nepotism are distinct problems in their own right, they are also mechanisms by which sexism and racism are continuously baked back into the system.

For example: Today, a disproportionate percentage of Blacks and Latinos come from economically disadvantaged families and attend underfunded public schools. As a result, a disproportionate number of Blacks and Latinos receive poor-quality educations and don't attend colleges and universities. This, in turn, justifies the "worries" of HR managers about the "intelligence" or "education" of minority employees. In short, the racism of generations past produced conditions that feed the classism of the present.

This synergistic interaction is even more pronounced when we combine racism and sexism with nepotism. That's because the widespread nepotism practiced in corporate America disproportionately affects the historically marginalized. If women and minorities were well represented in the corridors of management, nepotism would still be a bad thing, but it wouldn't grease the wheels of a racist and sexist system. Because white men have historically dominated the halls of power, white men who hire and promote their friends and relatives instead of seeking out the best talent are drawing water from the same discriminatory well that their forefathers did.

There are few (if any) reliable statistics on nepotism, but if my conversations and experiences are any indication, it's rampant. Said Chris Michel, "At that same place [as mentioned above], the CEO and the head of HR were married. Optics aside, from a legal perspective alone it was crazy that this well-known firm, with billions of dollars under asset, would do this. The irony is that this head of HR would often speak before women's groups about her ascent of the corporate ladder, which she ascribed to hard work. Meanwhile, the women in the audience had to keep from choking on their beverages because of her lack of awareness or the fact that she just didn't care."

Coworkers who have worked together in the past routinely promote each other as they climb the ladder. It's also not unusual to find fathers and children working for the same organization. The latter occurs because executives consistently circumvent the spirit of their companies' internship programs by fast-tracking their kids—and their friends' kids—through what should be a competitive process. Later, a certain percentage of the former interns are brought back, postgraduation, for permanent full-time positions.

What's most frustrating is then having to listen to these executives complain about not having enough diverse candidates who meet the criteria for full-time employment. One of those criteria is, of course, prior experience with a top firm, which these diverse candidates didn't receive because they were squeezed out of the internship programs by the children of the current executives. Despite their denials, many managers are deliberately ensuring the survival of the good ole boy network.

In addition to propping up a broken system, another consequence of unfair or discriminatory hiring, compensation, and promotion practices is the toll they take on employee minds and bodies. In the world at large, most humans enter fight-or-flight mode when confronted with threats to their safety or their ego. In the corporate world, neither option is acceptable. Because of this, "the workplace is . . . the perfect petri dish for growing cultures of fear, anxiety, competition, isolation, and threat." As a result, the average employee reacts to threats by internalizing the stress generated by these threats—stress that can negatively affect both their psychological and physical health.[19]

Among people who are repeatedly subjected to discriminatory behavior, one of the most common effects is a significant loss of confidence and self-esteem, sometimes called "imposter syndrome," which prompts the victims to believe that they are being denied job opportunities, pay raises, or promotions because they don't deserve them. They may come to believe that they're imposters masquerading as qualified candidates for the job, salary raise, or promotion.

During my interview with Rahsan Boykin, he described one of his own encounters with discrimination and imposter syndrome. "When I was a law student at Fordham, I got an interview with a partner a top New York City based law firm, which was arranged by the Black lawyer student association affiliated. The first question out of [the interviewer's] mouth was, 'How did you get here?' I responded with, 'Excuse me?' Thinking he was referring to my mode of transportation. He then said, 'How did you get the interview?' His attitude, posture, and previous line of questioning took the air out of my sails. I explained that I got the interview through the national Black lawyer association. 'That explains it,' he said, tossing my résumé to the side. He never referenced my résumé again as we went through the motions of a job interview.

"In that moment I was crushed, but I remember telling myself to hold it together. Needless to say I didn't get the job. That interaction shook my confidence immensely, forcing me to question whether I belonged as a lawyer at that level, giving me a form of . . . imposter syndrome. A few years later, ironically, I ended up landing a job at that same firm that had rejected me. The law firm that I ended up working with was the same firm that I initially applied coming out of law school. I never saw the partner again who had initially interviewed me, but I will remember that interview for as long as I live. Racism in corporate America is not about pejorative terms. It's more about 'he doesn't look like my cousin.' The hardest struggle of my career has always been getting a fair chance from people who didn't look like me. Funny enough, that changed when i joined Google. It was the first place I felt like I had a real opportunity go grow based on merit. And I think that was totally due to the values championed by the legal leadership team which consisted of a substantial number of women and minorities."

What can you do when you or someone you know is a victim of discrimination? And how exactly do you go about identifying and actually proving discrimination?

Here's what my colleagues and I did, all those years ago, in the wake of that London banker's racist outburst. We waited in our department until morning in order to file a complaint with the senior department leader (who happened to be a white woman). After she arrived, the six of us explained what had happened. She was in disbelief. Then she asked if we had any witnesses. What the . . . ? Now, *we* were in disbelief. After working through the night, all six of us had waited for an hour or two past the end of our shifts to report this horrendous behavior, and our leader didn't believe us. What I later realized was that she *did* believe us. She just didn't want to deal with escalating the issue.

In response to the second most egregious racist incident that I ever encountered, the one involving the regional leader in Asia, my approach was different. In that case, I had already complained about the man on two prior occasions, and nothing had been done. For that reason, and for the reasons listed next, I decided not to report him for a third time. To start, this manager had been with the firm for decades, during which time he'd cultivated an expansive internal network within the senior executive ranks. Hence, it would be my word against his, and even though many people were aware of his questionable character, he had the relationships to insulate himself from any repercussions. I did not. If his friends decided to launch a smear campaign against me, I would be the one to suffer and, most likely, any HR investigation would go nowhere.

Ultimately, I decided not to die on that particular hill.

It was more important to fight another day. As one of the few Black executives at the firm, someone who was willing to champion diversity and equity, I believed it was more important for me to hang around and serve as a buffer against guys like this than to make a brave but doomed gesture. This manager was a card-carrying member of the good ole boys club. He was abusive and, at times, a little too "friendly" with the company's young female employees. I was better off running interference and fighting the battles I *could* win. Although I did my best, before leaving the organization, to shield my matrix reporting employees from that manager, I feel that I failed them to some extent, and that the company failed us all. As I look back, however, I still believe that playing the long game was the right choice.

Sadly, most victims of discrimination are afraid to say or do anything for fear of retaliation, and rightly so. Regardless of what most companies say about confidentiality, whistleblower protections, and their prohibitions against retaliation, the reality is that retaliation happens all too frequently. No official policy is guaranteed to prevent retaliation because it's almost as hard to prove that you were punished for speaking up about discrimination as it is to prove that the discrimination actually happened. I've personally witnessed acts of retaliation on two occasions—and these occurred at companies that were listed as "top companies" for minorities in a variety of diversity publications.

If you believe you're a victim of discrimination, and you decide to ignore the risks and do something about it, your first task is to collect credible evidence of the discrimination. How can you prove that your failure to get a raise, promotion, or the like is based on an ism, especially if the discrimination isn't blatant?

Answer: It isn't easy, especially if your firm doesn't have clearly communicated policies, procedures, and guidelines to govern hiring, promotion, and compensation. Salaries in corporate America are not published, so most of you will have no idea of what your peer-level colleagues are earning unless you have a connection in HR who leaks the information. However, when you're applying for a new role, you *do* have a right to ask, "What's the salary range for that particular job grade/job range?" Keep in mind, though, that salary ranges per functional area can vary significantly. For example, if you're working in a support role, don't expect to make the same salary as your peer who has a revenue-generating role.

If, given the evidence, you're convinced that you're the victim of discrimination, what are your options for moving forward? Viable options?

Here, the answer depends on whom you ask. I posed this question to a number of experts. At one end of the scale, Rahsan Boykin said, "You have zero options. . . . You're stuck, and here's why. Where can you realistically go to get assistance? HR? And run the risk of being labeled as the complainer? Good luck trying to get a promotion after complaining about being the Black guy or the Latina or the Asian guy. If you get fired as a Black person, can you sue? Sure. But do you want to get another job? The only time I've seen a person in that situation move on successfully is when they were a high-level executive with a strong résumé, track record, and network to leverage. As a junior manager or someone working your way up from support services, it will be incredibly difficult."

At the other end of the scale are the experts who recommend a graduated, step-by-step approach like the one below. (It's "graduated" in that each subsequent step is a more serious escalation than the previous one, and each succeeding step is only undertaken if the previous one didn't produce a satisfactory resolution.)

1. Follow the process outlined in the employee handbook.
2. File a complaint with HR.
3. Hire an attorney to represent you in meetings with HR and/or company executives and arrange for alternative dispute resolution (ADR).
4. If necessary, have your attorney file a lawsuit.
5. File a complaint with the Equal Employment Opportunity Commission (EEOC).

Much of the time, however, this approach won't get results. The harsh reality is that the current system was not designed to benefit historically marginalized people. A big exception is when there's compelling written, audio, or video evidence of wrongdoing. Unfortunately, most perpetrators of discrimination are not reckless enough to leave a paper trail (or an electronic one).

Even with strong evidence on your side, the process is lengthy. A multi-billion-dollar corporation will have far deeper pockets than you—financial and legal resources against which you can't hope to compete. You should also know that if you file a complaint with the EEOC, the process typically takes between

1.5 and 2.5 years. That's for moving the case from the informal stage to a final resolution, assuming there is no appeal.[20]

The additional point of consideration is that cancel culture can kick in simply when an employee follows the outlined protocol by filing an EEOC complaint to protect rights that may have been violated. The employee's name may be published, along with the name of the institution they are bringing charges against. The irony here is that very few people will stop patronizing the services of the accused company, but the employee is silently canceled. Just for utilizing the process that was designed to assist in such matters.

A final option—one that's gaining momentum among African American executives—is to simply quit the rigged Corporate Game and launch your own business. In other words, "If you can't join 'em, beat 'em." For executives tired of trying to squeeze into an artificially narrow talent pipeline, opting out of corporate America has become an increasingly attractive option, with "talented but frustrated Black executives leaving big firms at an alarming rate." In today's digitally enabled entrepreneurial environment, there are more human *and financial* resources available to younger talent who want to advance their career goals on their own terms.[21]

"I am done with trying to forcefully navigate minorities to get Black people in senior levels," said Rahsan Boykin. "I have given up participating on diversity councils that are window dressing, because I'm tired of begging. I've shifted my focus from the fight to get people on to corporate boards . . . to supporting more Black entrepreneurs—funding and supporting minority owned enterprises. At this point it doesn't even matter what industries those enterprises are in as long as the companies are led by like minded, qualified people who are interested in bettering themselves and the community.

"Begging and hoping simply has not worked."

Boykin's advice to African Americans and other minorities who are frustrated with their career paths is to "join as many industry organizations as possible to build your network. Start networking in your local community or city with other diverse professionals that have similar interest. This network will be your support base when you come to the end of your corporate runway—be it five, ten, fifteen, or twenty years from now. Perhaps you can leverage them for VC money or tech advice, or even serve on the board of your start-up. My father always said, "you will only be able to go as far as the relationships you keep." He was right.

Corporate Diversity and Inclusion Programs

In an effort to create a true meritocracy, one based on a genuinely competitive talent marketplace that includes women and minorities, many corporations have developed diversity and inclusion programs. With few exceptions, however, these programs have achieved very little. True, they've generated more awareness around diversity, but talk is cheap. Moreover, these efforts often feel disingenuous, especially when the same people who enable discrimination are put in charge. And in some cases, the programs are nothing but Potemkin villages that managers can point to whenever they want to demonstrate "progress."

I have had a number of conversations over the years with several chief diversity officers (CDOs) who were frustrated with the lack of support they received from their CEO and executive leadership team. A telltale sign is the level to which a CDO reports, in one instance as low as five levels from the CEO. Many CDOs had been appointed to their role after a scandal or after the company's diversity metrics had come to light. They entered the role with high expectations but with a budget and staff not commensurate to the immediate expectations of the role.

The irony of it all is that not enough exposure has been given to the number of CDOs who have cycled in and then out of these roles before they can deliver on the lofty goals they were assigned. More often than not, the senior management team's commitment to change does not match the rhetoric and platitudes. After the George Floyd public lynching, LinkedIn overflowed with posts from some of the most iconic brands pledging their commitment to change, and pledging an increased investment in their Black employee population. Now, when they have been asked for their progress toward these pledges to be audited by third parties, we hear their excuses about their inability to find Black talent. Corporate executive Keith Wyche published his fourth book to address just that issue: *Diversity Is Not Enough: A Roadmap to Recruit, Develop, and Promote Black Leaders in America*. I expect that every CDO who has heard that excuse would bring Keith in for a fireside chat with their leadership team. After all, when you don't have the answers to systemic issues, you bring the thought leadership. In October of 2021, Citi made a public announcement stating its commitment to conducting a third-party racial equity audit, which will deepen its diversity, equity, and inclusion promises as it continues to address the racial wealth gap.

Personally, I find that serving on corporate diversity task forces and opining on the effectiveness of any one program has become challenging work. I say that because doing so places me in a position of having to juggle between the ideal and the reality, and I'm tired of being a pawn caught in that tension. On one hand, my presence validates the program, but on the other hand, because I'm an outspoken advocate of diversity, especially cultural and racial, the folks whose respect I've earned over a couple of decades expect that something meaningful and impactful will get done, that it won't be another check-the-box exercise or camouflage a reprioritization. But without the committed support of the leadership team, my involvement in reality may make little difference in the effectiveness of the program.

Before you express what I consider to be misplaced rage and what-about-me syndrome, consider thoroughly educating yourself on the very complicated history of Black people and women in this country, both within and outside corporate America. Stop feeling offended because your colleagues have been historically overlooked and set back by systems approved by this government, which has the ability to advance one group over another. I'm not throwing shade—it's simply a reality that we must continue working through in a unified manner to achieve the ideals we aspire to.

Can You Make a Difference?

If you're facing a workplace rampant with isms, and you decide not to opt out, is there anything you can do right now to help create a workplace that is more equitable and just? Yes, but just know that any results may take time. Among other things, you should consider the following action steps:

- Writing Glassdoor.com reviews about the companies where you've worked and where you've interviewed
- Building advocacy through the employee resource groups
- Voicing your concerns in employee engagement surveys
- When asked, submit D&I-related questions to the CEO and other members of the executive leadership team before a town hall. (Ask for specifics relative to timelines, metrics, and projected impact.)

If you own your company's stock, please know that you have these six rights as a common shareholder:

1. Voting power
2. Ownership
3. The right to transfer ownership
4. Dividends
5. The right to inspect corporate documents
6. The right to sue for wrongful acts

Use these rights to advance the cause of justice and fairness. With ownership comes power, including the power to change things for the better.

Dr. Errol Pierre on Employee Resource Groups and the Power of Out-of-the-Box Thinking

Errol Pierre is the SVP of State Programs for Healthfirst, New York's largest not-for-profit health insurer, with 1.6 million customers and 4,500 employees.

CJ: You once mentioned that you started an employee resource group (ERG).

EP: Correct. It was at Anthem, the parent company of Empire BlueCross BlueShield.

CJ: What was the ERG for—race, gender, shared interests?

EP: Age and/or corporate experience. It was called HYPE: Healthcare Young Professional Exchange. At the time, age seemed to be my most limiting factor in the workplace. I was perceived as "too young" to be a director and had to wait five years to be a VP based on feedback from my supervisor.

CJ: At what stage of your career was this?

EP: I was a "consultant"—essentially, an individual contributor with three to five years of work experience. In the next five to seven years, my next step would be manager. It would take ten years before I was even considered for a vice president role, which was too long for me. I had a fifteen- to eighteen-year plan to get to a C-suite role, and I was being very deliberate about how to do it.

CJ: What benefit did the ERG provide to its members and the company?

EP: I created the ERG to provide exposure for entry-level to senior-level employees. We started a mentoring program and a job shadowing program for associates who were considered too young to be paired with more experienced associates. We advocated for a more inclusive, multigenerational workforce. We also provided a resource to the company for perspectives about millennial consumers. When it comes to health insurance, young people tend not to buy it. So we created an internal focus group where the marketing and strategy departments could run ideas by us to get our perspectives. Lastly, we provided an opportunity for entry-level associates to gain "management" experience. By being a co-chair of a committee or a "site lead" in their respective states, they were part of the ERG leadership team. As such, when applying for management roles for the first time, they were able to point to their ERG leadership, even if they didn't have leadership experience in their current jobs.

CJ: Is the ERG still in existence? If so, is it thriving?
EP: Yes! My ERG actually became two different ERGs due to its size! HYPE remained for people focused on careers in healthcare, and MERGE was created as a "Multigenerational ERG." More than ten thousand associates from every corner of our organization—including nearly a quarter of Anthem's leaders—participate in at least one of our ten associate resource groups (ARGs). These groups offer associates meaningful opportunities to connect, collaborate, and grow. They add cultural insight to Anthem's business initiatives and help us cultivate deep ties with our

communities. HYPE was one of the first ERGs. It led to many others, and we paved the way for other employees to start ERGs. For example, I helped the founder of ACE (Asians Committed to Excellence) start their group.

CJ: What did the ERG do for your brand?

EP: I had exposure to the chief diversity officer of Anthem, who became a champion for me, talking in the rooms I couldn't get into. I also gained exposure to senior leaders. Two executive sponsors now knew my name and advocated for me. When our mentorship program caught on, the HR department decided to create an official program, and I was chosen to be a mentee in the inaugural program. I was partnered with high-level business executives two years in a row. I was also placed in Anthem's leadership program, which helped grow my business acumen. I ended up meeting thousands of associates. At the time, Anthem had thirty thousand employees. I knew most of the younger employees and was used as a resource to help people navigate their careers. This made me a hot commodity within the company. I was quickly promoted to a director-level position.

CJ: Did you feel a sense of accomplishment?

EP: Yes. The fact that the ERG is still there is awesome. That's how you leave a legacy.

CHAPTER NINE

Selfless Leadership

There's an important concept in Buddhism known as *No Self* that is frequently misinterpreted. Too often, *No Self* is thought to mean that we humans are an illusion—we don't really exist or (if we *do* exist) we're merely a bundle of data points who "strut and fret our hour upon the stage" in a computer simulation.

In reality, *No Self* is not about illusion but *delusion*. It's about the delusion of believing that each of us is a permanent, fixed entity who exists independently of everyone else. What *No Self* actually states is: None of us is an island. None of us is a self-contained entity. Think about it for a moment. Did you give birth to yourself? Do you feed yourself by willing wheat seeds into existence, and then nurturing the plants until they bear more wheat seeds that you grind into flour with equipment that you also willed into existence? At its core, *No Self* is about the *interdependence* of all people and things.

Sadly, many of us forget how much we depend on our fellow humans as well as on the earth itself. We behave as though we're living inside a vacuum composed entirely of our own ego.

This forgetfulness is the core problem with many corporate leaders. They've forgotten that a corporation is nothing but a legal construct. The only thing *real* about any organization is the people who interact with it—be they executives, employees, customers, or community members.

Worse: Many executives have *deluded* themselves into believing they can lead their companies in ways that are self-centered or self-aggrandizing without inflicting harm on employees, customers, the societies in which they live, and ultimately themselves. Instead of practicing *selfless leadership* by striving to achieve the greatest good for the greatest number of people, they practice ego-based leadership, aiming to enrich themselves. (Note that *ego* is merely the Latin word for *I*.) Today, the consequences of these *I*-based delusions are piling up—in the form of climate change, pollution, racism, inequality, and so on. The only solution is selfless leadership—a "we"-based form of leadership that recognizes our dependence on one another.

Characteristics of Selfless Leadership

When I returned to Citibank, I was assigned a new manager after only six weeks on the job. Even so, my original manager maintained a regular one-to-one meeting schedule with me. He did this because he was mindful that my hiring might look like a bait and switch. But mostly, he was a considerate leader, someone who cared about my well-being, even though I was no longer his responsibility.

Years earlier, by contrast, when my hiring manager was transferred six months after I joined the large global insurer (in the midst of the 2008 financial crisis), my new managers made little effort to tap my talents and experience. Either they had no interest in doing so, because they hadn't hired me, or they lacked talent management skills. Later, my original hiring manager, Bob Noddin, now the CEO of AIG Japan, requested that I join him in Asia to conduct an assessment of an $8 billion book of business. Were there other people capable of doing it? Of course. But he was looking to validate me. He felt bad for recruiting me to a company where the wheels were coming off. He wanted me to know that although I no longer reported to him, he wouldn't leave me high and dry.

These hiring managers displayed a key characteristic of selfless leadership: *doing your best to fulfill your promises to people.* Selfless leaders never throw their subordinates under the bus or treat them as "collateral damage." Although selfless leaders must strive to meet the company's goals, they don't do it at the expense of their people. They understand that every leader has a role to play in nurturing the company's most precious asset: people. Ego-based leaders view employees as fungible assets. Selfless leaders view them as *humans*, as well as resources.

Thanks to the example of these leaders, I always maintain an interest in my former employees, wherever they go. It thrills me when they reach out to pick my brain or share a success story. It's the kind of legacy I want to leave behind. And that's a second trait of selfless leaders: *They are mindful of their legacies.* They aren't in this game for short-term gain, but to leave a positive piece of themselves behind—even if that "piece" is simply a few words of advice that a former mentee occasionally recalls.

Another characteristic of the selfless leader is *belief in a code of ethics.* A good leader understands that they will sometimes have to make tough decisions. They will have to make judgment calls that may not be popular, but they will make those calls anyway because it's the right thing to do. For them, doing the right thing is paramount. Taking a stand may not bring material rewards, but they know they'll be able to look at themselves in the mirror. Most people recognize and appreciate this authentic leadership, especially during challenging times.

Finally, selfless leaders *take charge of guiding and coaching employees*, using techniques that boost people's confidence instead of crushing it. Even if the leader believes that an idea or strategy you've proposed is idiotic, they will respond by saying, "Okay, but have you also considered X?" instead of stomping on your feelings. This is a critical approach for developing talent. It demonstrates that the manager is committed not only to leading but also to developing the careers of the individual team members.

The way forward is for more leaders to understand how authentic, egoless leadership benefits everyone. After all is said and done, service to others is more important—and far more lasting—than a job title. Your role is not the main reason you appeared on the planet at this time. It's not the ultimate achievement during that dash from the day you were born to the day you cease to exist as a physical being. At the end of this life, it won't matter if your PowerPoint presentations were beautiful, if you kissed your bosses' asses to their satisfaction, if you won employee-of-the-month awards or received every promotion you ever wanted. The only thing that will matter is what kind of person you became and what you did to improve other people's lives.

Toward a *Genuine* Meritocracy

Webster's defines **meritocracy** as "a system, organization, or society in which people are chosen and moved into positions of success, power, and influence on the basis of their demonstrated abilities and merit."

During my thirty-plus-year career, the gap between this definition and the reality on the ground has become wide and wider. True meritocracy has taken a backseat to a relationship-based system (which one can convincingly argue was the "real system" all along). Genuine meritocracy *does* exist in isolated pockets of corporate America, thanks to the values and integrity of certain leaders and the cultures they have shaped, but it's far from common. In order to flourish, meritocratic values must flow from the top. Unless senior leadership commits to meritocratic principles and puts them into practice, meritocracy is nothing but a word—a veneer laid over a system based on personal relationships instead of results and performance-based data.

Leaders who consistently enable relationships to trump performance lack integrity, and as a consequence, their organizations lack a solid foundation for sustainable growth. Selfless leaders don't care who you know when it comes time to make hiring, promotion, and compensation decisions. For this reason, they do more than pay lip service to diversity, equity, and inclusion programs. They will not, for example, "address" a glaring deficiency in the organization's racial balance by hiring a few token minorities and then declaring: "Problem solved." A selfless leader will tackle the issue head-on.

Selfless leaders are true meritocrats, not because they necessarily believe that meritocracy is the best system ever devised for allocating human resources but because it's the only (existing) system that prioritizes *results*—and selfless leaders are nothing if not results-oriented. For them, the goal of leadership is not to maximize their own wealth and happiness. It's about how they and their teams can collectively accomplish the organization's objectives. To this end, they are all about optimizing their human resources to achieve the company's mission, which is why they couldn't care less about who your friends are, where you come from, and what you look like. They care only about how *you*—and your skills, knowledge, and experience—can contribute to the final outcome. When the success of a leader is measured by how well they organize and motivate their people to accomplish goals, the selfless leader usually comes out on top. In the process, this manager instills in their employees a results-oriented, meritocratic value system.

During this journey toward a genuine meritocracy, selfless leaders also experience real satisfaction from developing the talents of individual team members.

My approach to leadership is, and has always been, to focus on the people I've been blessed to lead. I look for their potential, while sharing the nuggets of wisdom I've accrued over my career, in an effort to uncover their inner superpowers. For me, the joy is in watching them evolve into a person/worker/leader capable of achieving great things.

As a leader, one of the greatest gifts you can share is your ability to see and value an individual's potential and character before either becomes obvious to most people. Leaders with this ability are better able to leverage the talent needed to build teams, initiatives, and entire organizations and to deliver superior quality. Ultimately, that's your role as a leader: to look down the field for opportunities to score and then assign the best people to the task.

Leaders who fail to do this aren't necessarily bad people. Some may simply not subscribe to my philosophical approach; others may have reached their limit relative to what they actually have to give. They can't offer you what they don't have.

Even the Best Leaders Are Fallible

I once worked under a manager who was truly awesome. He firmly believed in always taking the high road. This manager cautioned me about being too judgmental of leaders and colleagues who exhibited questionable behavior. He advised me to assume that people usually did things with the best of intentions. Inspired by his code of ethics, I respected that advice, and I've since tried to follow his code of ethics because it represents the corporate America I want to live in. It's a vision in which hard work pays off and where employee value, customer value, and shareholder value are held in the same regard.

I respected that man as a leader. He exuded integrity and inspired me with his thoughtfulness. His top priority was always the greater good. Because of that, and because he was fair, people worked harder for him. I would run through a brick wall for him, not that he would ever ask such a thing, because I wanted him to win. He believed that leaders should keep their promises—and when those promises couldn't be kept, it was the leader's responsibility to apologize, explain why the promise had been broken, and outline how he or she would do better in the future. To this day, I hear his voice when I witness bad behavior or smell bullshit: "Curtiss, these are your leaders [or colleagues], so assume the best intentions."

In the intervening years, however, I decided to modify his advice to "assume but verify."

As a leader, remember that what employees do over the course of days or weeks is not the whole of who they are. Any missteps made during that time—assuming they *are* missteps and not a long-term pattern of behavior—should not overshadow an entire year's worth of good effort, much less an entire career's worth. Treat missteps as teachable moments, episodes from which you can draw lessons to pass along to the next generation of leaders.

Dr. Maya Angelou once said: "When you get, give. When you learn, teach." Create a mentoring "lesson plan" drawn from your ever-growing archive of teachable moments. Hopefully, your employees, mentees, colleagues (and even other managers) will absorb some of this wisdom. Over time, the "students" may not recall the origin of these lessons, but the words will resonate over the course of their lifetimes.

Leaders are human. Even the best are perfectly imperfect. On certain days, it may be all they can do to get out of bed because they're feeling physically or mentally unwell. Maybe all they have to give that day is a phony smile that pisses you off. Here is where *you*, as a selfless leader in training, can flip the script and try to see the best in them. You might offer a few uplifting words of gratitude—a simple "thank you for your leadership" as you close out an email. Not every leader is a Bill Clinton who's capable of making everyone in the room feel good as soon as he arrives, so don't expect this of your managers. (And don't place all your hopes or faith in someone simply because the person is a member of your gender or race, or shares your sexual orientation.)

Always remember: *You* have the ability to control your destiny and shape the leadership landscape of the company by embracing selfless leaders and their philosophies. If you earn their trust, they will share their vulnerabilities, allowing you to see that even the best leaders are in a perpetual state of development. And then, at an appropriate time, leaders vested in your development will also provide you with proximity to power, allowing you to see the inner workings of things. In turn, you will be positioned to make better decisions. This approach builds confidence and creates a culture of trust and collaboration. People will perform in a way that makes them feel good, while delivering results. A good leader will listen to, and value, your informed opinion, empowering you to excel.

Avoid leaders who expect followers to shrink themselves in order for them to feel more important. The path to leadership is not about shrinking others. It's about elevating others. It's about appreciating that everyone has a backstory. Sometimes you're meant to be in the starring role; other times, you're meant to be in a supporting role. Both are critical to the process as long as there is a deliberate focus on the greater good.

Good leaders understand that there's nothing wrong with being a supporting player. They put their egos aside and, when appropriate, allow their subordinates to take the starring role, or they revise the script to create additional opportunities for them. In addition, they always make themselves available for counsel, guidance, and advocacy. These leaders survey the cast with a wide-angle lens to ensure that they are managing objectively and fairly, avoiding the microinequities that can lead to an oppressive culture.

I believe we all stand on the shoulders of those who came before us and, therefore, we have a moral debt that needs to be paid forward. Your performance as a leader can be viewed as the return on the time, prayers, patience, wisdom, and energy that your ancestors invested in the family's future. (I'm eternally grateful for what my ancestors invested in my future.) A fitting way to honor those who came before us is to model the best possible leadership behavior, striving to create an environment of fairness and high ethical standards as we work to make the world a better place.

That's a legacy worth having.

That's something for which you'll be fondly remembered.

Conclusion

Over the years, I've mentored and coached an untold number of bright, ambitious, kind, and considerate people, helping them to manage their corporate careers toward success, however they defined it. One of my superpowers is discovering unacknowledged talents and ability and then helping them amplify it in their life so they can strategically bring more of their true self to the table.

In this book, I promised I'd show you how to navigate the corporate landscape and achieve career success without losing yourself along the way. It turns out, the climb on the corporate ladder is not always a straight shot. Sometimes you have to go sideways. Other times, hanging out in one spot for years is exactly where you'll want to be. At some point you might even abandon your journey through corporate America altogether. Staying in is a choice.

And there is power in choice.

You get to decide what kind of person you'll be in work and in life. As my mentor says, "You don't have to roar to be lion." You don't need to be strong and wrong. You need to be you, a you you've empowered with knowledge so you're walking into corporate America with eyes open.

You shouldn't feel like you have to compromise your principles and values to secure a good job and a good future for yourself. Bad managers allow bad culture, but this is only an imaginary impediment in front of you. The ripple effects of your authenticity and integrity in the workplace, along with others', will build into a tsunami that can wash away the evils of the corporate business world that threaten to consume decency and humanity.

You are a future leader in our shared business world. I'll feel I've done my job if you take away from this book a plan to strategically navigate your corporate career in a way that leaves the workplace—and the world—a better place behind you. You decide what you want to get out of this journey.

I just want to remind you of a few things to keep in mind as you push ahead. You'll need to expand how you think of yourself. You have to make a living, yes, but it's not all about the dollars. If you think advancement and success are measured in treasure, fewer opportunities will come your way.

But good financial planning does allow freedom, so be smart about who you want to be and what you'll put up with from managers, coworkers, and policies to earn that coin. And always have some money set aside so that you can walk out of a bad situation.

You will need different things at different times of your life; you are, after all, a human being, not a human been. Know that you are still evolving wherever you are in your career. Don't let any job, no matter how fancy the title, define who you are.

Remember, you have a life outside work, so never forget to cultivate your interests and passions beyond your desk.

Corporations are great places to learn about yourself, to learn discipline and strategy and how to nurture good, in yourself and in those around you. Be open to learning, even from some of the unscrupulous characters you meet. (Sometimes the most profound lessons come from the most unexpected sources.)

Build the corporate world you want to live in. Surround yourself with others who believe in you and are honest with you.

The world needs more leaders-in-training like you. The time for tiptoeing around corporate America, quietly conforming to the tacit standards of behavior and leadership, the existing understanding of success, is behind us. Now, together, we must tackle the opportunity we have to reshape the workplace and how it's managed to bring in more humanity.

This movement starts with one person—you.

Acknowledgments

This book would not have been possible without my brother Ralph, who from the various stages of my life has been my protector, my provider, and my counselor, introducing me to the possibilities of a career in corporate America, and life in general.

I am also grateful to the iconic corporations and organizations that have allowed me to pressure test the theory that I learned in school while applying my personal philosophy of leadership on global projects, large-scale operations, task force teams, consulting engagements, and in the boardroom over the last thirty-plus years.

To the leaders Jerry George, Ling Li, Dwight Carter, Richard Mariso, Sonia Alleyne, Kathleen Osborne, Kevin Sack, Keith Wyche, Robert Noddin, Murli Buluswar, Phillip Cormie, and Ralph Cleveland, who trusted me enough by being vulnerable and transparent so that I learned, and not just met, but exceeded my potential—thank you for your leadership.

Thank you for your mentorship, guidance and scriptures, and for opening your homes and sharing your families, honoring the fact that I am more than just a corporate employee and certainly more than the title that was associated with my name in the corporate directory. I've had a lot of managers over the course of my career, but your humanity and loyalty rang true. I take a piece of you with me into every business decision.

To all the individuals that I have had the opportunity to lead and more importantly, serve, thank you for trusting my vision, stepping up when I asked for ideas, and pushing me to grow.

Thank you to members of my Pitney team: Justin, Kelly-Ann, Zameer, Cassandra, Renette, Yamiuris, and Gerald.

Thanks to my entire RCS team at AIG, who, by virtue of their commitment to our shared vision and mastery in the art of followership enabled me to lead and deliver some outstanding outcomes.

To my assistants Samuel Lahoz, Priscilla Vega, Lillian Padilla, Barbara Hacke, Tiffany Murchison, Almalina Ledsma, and Patrice Hall, thank you for keeping me organized over the years.

To Renee, thanks for your work ethic and dedication to excellence.

To Jai Dorsey, thanks for being the type of selfless and authentic leader who understands the importance of sponsorship.

Thank you Thusanda Duckett for bringing your true, an authentic-self to the arena. You are exactly what corporate America needs as a CEO. Yes, it can be done!

To my founding gallery director, Paula Coleman, you were a godsend. Understanding that my sixty-hour workweek and business travel were obstacles to getting our gallery open, you made it happen.

To Lawrence and Carol Finney thanks for your love, inspiration and support of me as a gallerist, and more importantly a human being.

To my friend and former business partner Vinod Raghavan, after tolerating enough of the corporate shenanigans, thanks for encouraging me to join you in starting our own consulting firm. It was a gratifying experience that I'll never forget.

For a first-time author, turning an idea into a book is as difficult as it sounds. However, I can now attest that the experience is both internally challenging and rewarding. I owe an enormous debt of gratitude to Susan Middleton for pushing me to stop talking and get to writing and for helping me develop the initial outline of this book. To Peter Gerardo, for adding your expertise in helping structure my content into a coherent story, giving it life. To Christina Palaia, thanks for adding your editorial and project management skills to this process, very much appreciated. To those who sat for interviews or provided me with detailed and constructive comments on one or more chapters, including Andres Alexander, Verna Ford, Richard Welsh, Susan Middleton, Matthew Lundy, Cynthia Hardy, Mark Smith, Christina Lucas, Rashaan Boykin, Bill Stephney, Tamara Nall, Leon Hampton, Tom Bridgeforth, Abdullah Sheikh, and Dr. Errol Pierre.

To "the boys," Jeff, O.T., Fred, and Chris, thanks for the daily text messages of encouragement and levity as we deal with being who we are in the corporate space.

To Fred Richardson: Who would have thought when we met as roommates in the New York State Police Academy that thirty-six years later we'd still be watching each other's backs in the corporate workplace?

To Curtiss Spinks and Don Singleman, we started as work colleagues and became brothers. Thanks for having a strong moral compass, sharing your families with me, and being my ears and voice in the room, in my absence.

To Andres Alexander: We met when you were an ambitious MBA student looking to get your foot in the door of corporate America. Now, after almost twenty years in the business trenches together, I thank you for never shying away from a challenge, and God knows there have been many.

To my Harlem connections, Curtis Archer and Clyde Williams, thank you for the sincere friendship, mentorship, wise counsel, and brotherhood. Thank you to the brotherhood of 100 Black Men of America. Special thanks to my mentors Dr. Louis Murdock, Phil Banks Sr., Curley Dossman, my wise counselors Adrian Stratton, Jarred Douglas, and Marvin Dickerson, and members of The Seven—Vernon, Acey, Bill, Charles, Kola, Jewett, and Bert—for having the courage to stand in the face of adversity for things that were not always popular but that you believed were proper. Look yourselves in the mirror every day and feel good about who you are.

Thank you to the entire ecosystem of friends, educators, and parents from my childhood neighborhood in the St. Albans–Jamaica section of Queens, New York. To Paul Hewitt and Rob Parker thanks for allowing me to vicariously live out my fantasies of being a basketball coach, and sport columnist through you guys . . . the old neighborhood did pretty good huh?

Thank you to my loving mother, Earthell Wittlinger, who taught me the importance of projecting style, culture, class, and competence throughout my life's journey. To Ulrich Wittlinger, thanks for your unwavering love for me, my mother, siblings, children, and grandchildren. To my baby sister, Zain, I hope this book makes you proud.

Finally, and most importantly, I want to thank my better half, Camille, for keeping our children organized, being patient, supporting my many endeavors, and sharing me with the world as I go through this uniquely complex but fulfilling journey that God has laid out for me. Thanks for tolerating the long business trips abroad and my many disappearances into my home office while trying to work through prioritization of my thoughts and planned actions. I know it's not easy, but I owe you a debt of gratitude for trusting me, believing in me, and loving me.

If I overlooked anyone, please blame it on my head and not my heart. . . . I thank you as well.

Notes

1. "71 Percent of HR Professionals Are Female," Recruiting Headlines, February 12, 2019, https://recruitingheadlines.com/71-percent-of-hr-professionals-are-female/.

2. Ibid.

3. Timothy Noah, "The Black Wage Gap Matters," New Republic, June 11, 2020, https://newrepublic.com/article/158142/black-wage-gap-income-inequality.

4. Tom Bridgeforth, "Exiting the Corporate Matrix," LinkedIn, March 6, 2017, https://www.linkedin.com/pulse/exiting-corporate-matrix-tom-bridgeforth-pmp/.

5. John Pencavel, "The Future Hours of Work?" Stanford Institute for Economic Policy Research, September 2018, https://siepr.stanford.edu/publications/policy-brief/future-hours-work.

6. Peter Kuhn and Fernando Lozano, "The Expanding Workweek? Understanding Trends in Long Work Hours among U.S. Men, 1979–2006," *Journal of Labor Economics* 26, no. 2 (April 2008), https://doi.org/10.1086/533618.

7. Daniel Markovits, "How Life Became an Endless, Terrible Competition," *The Atlantic*, September 2019, https://www.theatlantic.com/magazine/archive/2019/09/meritocracys-miserable-winners/594760/.

8. Ibid.

9. Ibid.

10. Kate Kelly and Lananh Nguyen, "Rookie Bankers Sour on Wall Street's Pitch of Big Pay and Long Hours," *New York Times*, July 26, 2021, https://www.nytimes.com/2021/07/26/business /investment-banking-work-life-balance.html.

11. *Racism at Work Survey Results*, Pearn Kandola, March 2018, https://pearnkandola.com/app/uploads/2018/03/RaceSurvey ReportFNLNewBrand.pdf.

12. Phil Wahba, "Only 19: The Lack of Black CEOs in the History of the Fortune 500," *Fortune*, February 21, 2021, https://finance .yahoo.com/news/only-19-lack-black-ceos-120000751.html.

13. Jessica Guynn and Brent Schrotenboer, "Why Are There Still So Few Black Executives in America?" *USA Today*, published August 20, 2020, updated February 4, 2021, https://www.usatoday.com /in-depth/money/business/2020/08/20/racism-black-america-corp orate-america-facebook-apple-netflix-nike-diversity/5557003002/.

14. Rachel Thomas, Marianne Cooper, Gina Cardazone, Kate Urban, Ali Bohrer, Madison Long, Lareina Yee, Alexis Krivkovich, Jess Huang, Sara Prince, Ankur Kumar, and Sarah Coury, *Women in the Workplace 2020*, McKinsey & Company and LeanIn .Org, September 30, 2020, https://wiw-report.s3.amazonaws.com /Women_in_the_Workplace_2020.pdf.

15. Rachel Thomas, Marianne Cooper, Ellen Konar, Ali Bohrer, Ava Mohsenin, Lareina Yee, Alexis Krivkovich, Irina Starikova, Jess Huang, and Delia Zanosch. *Women in the Workplace 2019*, McKinsey & Company and LeanIn.Org, 2019, https://wiw-report .s3.amazonaws.com/Women_in_the_Workplace_2019.pdf.

16. Stephen Miller, "Black Workers Still Earn Less Than Their White Counterparts," SHRM, June 11, 2020, https://www.shrm.org

/resourcesandtools/hr-topics/compensation/pages/racial-wage
-gaps-persistence-poses-challenge.aspx.

17. Bailey Reiners, "57 Diversity in the Workplace Statistics You
    Should Know," Builtin.com, October 20, 2021, updated October
    27, 2021, https://builtin.com/diversity-inclusion/diversity-in-the
    -workplace-statistics.

18. Stephanie Marcus, "Mary Tyler Moore Tackled the Wage Gap on
    Her Show Back in 1972," *Huffington Post*, January 25, 2017, https:
    //www.huffpost.com/entry/mary-tyler-moore-tackled-the-wage
    -gap-on-her-show-back-in-1972_n_58890e0ee4b061cf898c867b.

19. Gareth Chick, "Corporate Traumatic Stress Disorder (CTSD) Is
    the Scourge of the 21st-Century Workplace," Training Industry,
    April 4, 2019, https://trainingindustry.com/blog/compliance
    /corporate-traumatic-stress-disorder-ctsd-is-the-scourge-of-the
    -21st-century-workplace/.

20. Kevin C. Crayon II, "EEO Complaints for Federal Employees—
    How Long Is the Process?" Crayon Law Firm, June 4, 2017, updated
    May 28, 2021, https://www.crayonlawfirm.com/post/2017/06/04
    /eeo-complaints-for-federal-employees-how-long-is-the-process.

21. Peter Lauria, "Why Is Black Talent 'Opting Out' of Corporate
    America?" *Briefings*, Korn Ferry, https://www.kornferry.com
    /insights/briefings-magazine/issue-44/why-is-black-talent-opting
    -out-of-corporate-america.

About the Author

Curtiss Jacobs, born in Savannah, Georgia, but a lifelong New Yorker, spent over thirty years working in the financial services sector in various senior leadership roles at such global companies as AIG, Pitney Bowes, Merrill Lynch, Bank of America, and Citigroup, where he developed and implemented transformation strategies to mitigate risk, improve global organizational efficiency and effectiveness, and drive growth globally.

Prior to his career on Wall Street, Curtiss was a successful fashion and celebrity photographer, honing his skills working as a full-time assistant under legendary photographers Richard Avedon and Annie Leibovitz. In 2009, he opened the doors to Renaissance Fine Art of Harlem (since rebranded Curtiss Jacobs Gallery), with the mission to provide exhibition and curatorial opportunities to underserved communities. He also cofounded and serves as managing partner of Uptown Advisory Group LLC (UAG), a boutique business management consultancy based in New York City, and recently rejoined Citigroup as transformation executive.

He is passionately committed to lifetime service and has served on the boards of 100 Black Men of America, World of

Money, Project Art, and other nonprofit organizations that focus on improving communities by investing in people through advocacy, scholarships, mentoring, education, access to health and wellness programs, and economic empowerment initiatives.

Curtiss earned a BS in Management and Communications from Adelphi University, where he now serves on the President's Advisory Council. He holds an MBA in International Business from Northeastern University in Boston.

Curtiss is an executive coach, public speaker, and lecturer on corporate career navigation, entrepreneurship, and matters of equity, diversity, and inclusion.

Curtiss lives in New York City.

CPSIA information can be obtained
at www.ICGtesting.com
Printed in the USA
BVHW042002020822
643584BV00004B/10/J